When Death Occurs

When Death Occurs

A Practical Consumer's Guide

FUNERALS

MEMORIALS

BURIAL

CREMATION

BODY DONATION

JOHN M. REIGLE

CONSUMER ADVOCATE PRESS

Consumer Advocate Press
P.O. Box 64
Curran, MI 48728

LCCCN: 2002090666

Reigle, John M.
    When death occurs : a practical consumer's guide
funerals, memorials, burial, cremation, body donation / John M. Reigle.—1st ed.
    p. cm.
    1. Funeral rites and ceremonies—United States—
Planning. 2. Death—Handbooks, manuals, etc.
I. Title.

GT3203.R45 2002   393'.0297
                                                         QBI02-20256

ISBN: 0-9716518-0-9

Printed in the United States of America

Success—Measured by Service

"Make no mistake that most of the so-called "Death Care Professionals" are in truth "Death Care Sales Persons" unwilling to forego the quick sale for the long-term good of the client, which is, of course, the essence of service. So which is it going to be? Do we measure success by our sales or by our service to others?"

THOMAS P. LYNCH*, Keynote Address
Michigan Funeral Directors Convention, May 7, 1998

* Owner of Lynch Funeral Home, Milford, Michigan.
Author of *The Understanding: Life Studies from the Dismal Trade, Still Life in Milford: Poems* and *Bodies in Motion and at Rest: On Metaphor and Mortality.*

CONTENTS

ACKNOWLEDGMENTS

Special thanks to the many people who helped make this book possible: the families who entrusted their loved ones to my service, and those who will someday use this information to care for a loved one.

Amy Cannello, who helped get me started with this book. Mary Gettler, Mary Ulrich, Lindsay Smolinski, Tom White, and attorney Dave Wecker, who believed in this as much as I, and for whom I am eternally grateful. Special remembrance and thanks go to my grandparents, John J. and Wanda E. Reigle both licensed funeral directors, who dedicated their lives to serving the "working man and his family" in Flint. My father, James B. Reigle, Walter Skinner, Florence Coleman, and Jim Montague, who instilled in me the ethic of serving all families with respect and dignity, regardless of financial status. My great aunt Charlene Browder, who provided 38 years of service to bereaved families, helping them deal with Social Security, Veterans, Probate Court, and much more. Her services after the funeral helped build a reputation of superior service that made Reigle Funeral Homes so successful.

Jack Hamady, whose life and unselfish dedication to his community and his country helped inspire me to do more for others. My mother, Maribeth Myers Reigle, who along with Cody, Babs, and O'Leary, provided shelter during the storms.

Rene Ortlieb, who wouldn't let me surrender, even when those around me had.

PART 1

Introduction

Choices for Better Living

Here are some suggestions to help yourself and others—before you plan for a funeral:

Long-Term Health Care Insurance (L.T.H.C.I.)

Most people are under the illusion that medicare will pay for their long-term health care services like nursing home or assisted living costs. They do not.

Long-Term Health Care Insurance can help to enhance the quality of life for a disabled person. If the services of a nursing home or in-home nursing support become a necessity, it can protect your life's savings from health care expenses.

If you are pre-planning a funeral to spare your survivors the financial or psychological burden—STOP—and find out if you have Long-Term Health Care Insurance. Most ordinary health insurance only pays for a limited period of time in a nursing home and may not cover expenses if you decide to be cared for in your own home. L.T.H.C.I. can protect family assets from being depleted by a stay in a nursing home (usually $5,000–$6,000 dollars per month) and may cover expenses for care in your own home. The financial burden avoided by having L.T.H.C.I. is much greater than that of prepaying a funeral. Check with insurance agents and compare coverage options.

Three companies you should compare for coverage and costs are: G.E., John Hancock, CNA.

Nor love thy life, nor hate;
but what thou liv'st
Live well; how long or
short permit to Heaven.
—JOHN MILTON
(from *Paradise Lost*)

National Organ Donation Hot Line at 1-800-24-DONOR.

Organ Donor Card

When you are pre-planning a funeral, take time to consider becoming an organ donor. Organ donation does not add to the cost of a funeral or limit an individual's choice of services. You could improve or save another person's life. Many states register organ donors through their drivers' license bureau. Find out how to become an organ donor, discuss organ donation with your family, and carry your organ donor card. Contact the National Organ Donation Hot Line at 1-800-24-DONOR.

Estate Planning

Because probate laws vary between states, it is very difficult to offer general advice for establishing a will or living trust. It is important to review your needs and wishes, and to consult with a professional. Shop carefully for an advisor—you need an accountant or attorney specializing in estate planning and tax law to discuss the options available to you in your state. By itemizing your assets, making a will, and determining in writing who gets what, you can avoid wasted time and money later in Probate Court. Proper planning with a living trust avoids unnecessary taxation and directs your property to those you choose—not the courts. Call the Center for the Avoidance of Probate at 800-338-0227 for more information.

Buyer Beware!

Any consumer purchasing anything can be taken advantage of if they are uninformed, under duress, or don't have the time to compare and shop for like goods and services. This is especially true when death occurs. The funeral industry finds its consumers uninformed, under duress, and without the time to compare. Furthermore, the industry has gone to great lengths to make it difficult to compare prices and identify who owns what businesses, and existing laws offer little protection against well-trained salespeople.

When death occurs, you probably won't find many businesses that will take the time to figure out exactly what you want, and then how to do it as affordably as possible. That's precisely the reason I wrote this book. Here are all of your options, my outlook on various traditions, and suggestions to help you find **services** that meet your needs.

The Industry Loves the Word Protective

Let's consider what happens to the deceased when death occurs, and the events that follow. Funeral homes, cemeteries, vault companies, and casket manufacturers have long sold the concept and importance of "protective" caskets and vaults. It is a natural act to protect the ones we love, and this industry goes all out to push that emotional button of "protection" when we die. Most consumers do not have enough information about the subject to question the industry in their attempt to sell such merchandise.

Autopsy

Consider the process when someone dies. An autopsy is performed to determine the cause of death followed by embalming to preserve the body so that viewing of the deceased and delayed burial or cremation is possible. After you die, the tender care once given to the "patient" or person ends. A complete autopsy includes the head being cut open and the brains examined. The internal organs are removed and examined and not always carefully put back in. It is not a pretty sight nor is it always necessary. Teaching hospitals strongly encourage autopsies to train their students, but rarely tell the families exactly how the process of an autopsy is performed. If the survivors were shown a video they would faint, and, unless law required it, not many would volunteer their dearly departed—unless, of course, they didn't like the deceased.

Embalming

If the family so chooses to view the deceased, it is the talents of the embalmer/funeral director that put the deceased person back together again. Embalming includes the process of making incisions on the lower neck, arms, and legs to access the arteries and veins. The embalmer injects chemicals into the arteries and drains the blood and excess embalming fluids out of the veins. An instrument called a trocar is used to pierce the internal organs; it is inserted near the naval and repeatedly forced throughout the abdomen to remove any excess fluids (it has suction capabilities) or any organic matter that can pass through its opening. The trocar is then used to inject chemicals into the internal organs to prevent any gasses or ill effects of decomposition from disrupting the viewing or funeral. To conclude the process, most of the body openings are either glued or sewn shut to prevent any leaking of fluids.

The Beautiful Corpse

Simply put, the deceased does not go from the hospital or nursing home right into the casket. The process of autopsy and embalming is much more graphic and gruesome than the general public has been told. If the public really saw what happened to the deceased, they might not see the "need" to purchase a "protective" casket and "protective" vault. What the public sees at a funeral is a well-groomed, made-up deceased that has been cut, injected, sewn, and changed from its natural state. This beautiful corpse image, created by the funeral director, sways the survivors into believing the need to keep "protecting" their loved one by purchasing what makes the industry very profitable: protective caskets and protective vaults. Buried bodies, whether embalmed or not, change. They decompose just as they were intended. Embalming allows for viewing and that's it.

So, Why Do We Do What We Do?

First of all, what are we protecting? A deceased that has been cut from stem to stern, injected with chemicals, sewn and glued shut, in a $3,000.00 casket? Or by purchasing a "protective vault" are we trying to protect a metal casket or lavish wood casket, that we just spent a month's salary on? A casket is really nothing more than a unique piece of furniture used for viewing the deceased, period. The purchase of an expensive casket sometimes inspires the purchase of a vault, **neither** of which helps the family recover from the grief or loss that they have suffered.

Vaults: What a RIP

Most vaults are placed in the grave and then the casket is placed in the vault, and finally the lid is placed on top of the base. Is the seal on the vault tested before the dirt is put on top of the vault? No. Is the seal of the vault buried beneath the frost line in Northern climates? No. Do you have any assurance that some dirt or grass doesn't stick to the lid before it is placed in the grave? No.

Now think about this: often vaults are placed in graves that already have water in them. The vault will float until the lid is placed on it and covered with dirt. The lid cannot sit firmly on the base to create a seal unless it is level, not floating, so water can seep into the vault before the lid has a chance to seal to the base. Vaults should be sealed above the ground and tested before they are buried if there is any guarantee or implied agreement that the vault is "protective". Usually they are not sealed above ground. If a vault priced at $800.00 is promised to be protective, why do they offer vaults that are thousands of dollars more? They are playing on the emotions of the bereaved, playing with your money, or promising something they can't deliver and can't be proved differently in the future without digging up the grave. The warranty on a "protective" vault is about as useless as putting perfume on a pig. The companies give themselves many ways out, and the consumer is at a huge disadvantage in proving their case.

Non-Protective Vaults

The general concept of putting a casket into a concrete container to prevent the grave from sinking is probably a good idea. If you consider that large cemeteries use heavy equipment to dig graves, place monuments, and mow the lawn, then a concrete container is ideal to keep the graves from sinking or collapsing. The cemeteries must add dirt and reseed graves that have sunk in order to maintain the appearance for visitors. Vaults ensure that the gravesite will remain in good condition for many years to come. In this country, once land is a grave it is always a grave, so maintenance at cemeteries is a concern.

Caskets

A casket is a unique piece of furniture. Period. They are used to show the deceased to the survivors and then buried or burned. No casket stops the decomposition of the deceased, and if it did, for what purpose? When caskets are promised to be "protective," remember what we do to the deceased when autopsied and embalmed. If you choose to purchase a casket, buy what you like to look at. Remember your loved ones with **services** that are meaningful, memorable, and valuable to the living.

For decades, the American consumer has expressed a need for plain and simple, inexpensive caskets. They have abandoned traditional funerals when all they had to choose from was lavish caskets and canned services, when plain and simple caskets with meaningful, memorable, valuable services to the living would do just fine.

Every effort is made to confuse the consumer, by changing names of caskets given them by manufacturers to avoid price comparisons, using separate showrooms, and offering few choices in the plain and simple price range. You will find most funeral homes offer a few inexpensive caskets, a few very expensive caskets, and the majority in the price range **they** want you to buy. It creates the illusion of what is average. Caskets are marked up 2 to 3 times their wholesale costs, and prices vary considerably between sellers

Shame, Shame, Shame

Perhaps the most shameful merchandising ploy is that used by a major casket company in many funeral homes. They offer a line of plain and simple "cremation caskets" that they recommend be sold in a separate showroom or from a book, **away from the traditional burial caskets**. This is last-ditch effort to get a family choosing cremation to buy something. This also keeps the plain and simple caskets away from the more lucrative burial customers, who would usually be shown more expensive caskets.

Remember this: The deceased who are buried do not derive any more benefit from their caskets than the deceased who are cremated. It is a matter of profit that funeral providers hide caskets that are plain, simple and less expensive from the lucrative burial customer.

Urns

The single most absurd product sold to consumers is the "protective" burial urn used for burying cremated remains, i.e. ashes, basic elements of the earth. No harm or change can become of ashes. Yet the industry, in hopes of making a huge profit, tries to sell "protective" vaults for urns and ashes. If ashes are buried, the grave will not change or sink, as a burial casket would without a basic concrete vault. If the grave were marked, why would it be disturbed, as the cemetery or funeral director might plead when selling you a "protective" burial urn?

There are very few requirements made to account for a family's disposition of ashes. Some states have laws that forbid scattering on public land. Before purchasing an urn, consider what you will be doing with the ashes. It is generally not necessary or required by law to purchase an urn for any method of disposition. Urns are mostly used for display, at home or in a niche at a Columbarium. If a crematory or funeral home insists that you purchase an urn, you may provide your own container or vase, probably for much less money than the cost of those offered.

Most crematories place the ashes in a plastic bag and then into a hard plastic box before giving them to the family or funeral director. *This container is suitable for burial and for holding the ashes until scattering is complete.*

Pre-Arrangements

Pre-**purchasing** a casket, vault, cemetery lot, or marker is a sad tactic used by this industry. They try to get you to believe that it is necessary and collect your money for merchandise and services before someone else does. This is sales-oriented, not service. Which is more important?

Pre-**planning**, considering all of your options with your survivors, loved ones, the people who will benefit from the funeral and memorial, is a good idea. The **survivors** should plan, and have a voice in pre-planning, and the wishes of all should be taken into consideration.

Pre-planning allows the survivors to "shop around," considering and comparing the various services and merchandise. Unless the monies are 100% refundable upon request (including interest earned) **then I do not encourage pre-payment**.

Pre-planning the service is a good idea. Thinking about the music, pictures, memorabilia, clergy, and family who may wish to participate is highly recommended. It is the thought and effort put into planning a meaningful, memorable, valuable service to the living that helps the survivors survive.

What to Look For in a Funeral Home

Not all funeral directors, funeral homes, cemeteries, and cremation societies fall short of meeting the needs of their clients. There are some outstanding individuals and companies that have evolved away from selling, focusing rather on serving the long-term needs of their clients. These people and their respective businesses provide services that are meaningful, memorable, and valuable to the consumers, the survivors—friends, family, and community. They are few and far between.

Funerals and memorials today can include the use of videotapes, pictures of loved ones, and when done properly, provide at least one-half hour of meaningful services, a sort of documentary of the life of the deceased. The love shown in the remembrance and tributes paid to the deceased during the **services** will be remembered longer than any casket, vault, or urn.

A funeral home should meet the following requirements:

- They should be able to create a meaningful, memorable, valuable service for the living. Their interest in gathering information about the deceased and combining it with pictures, flowers, music, and religious ceremony is essential in creating a funeral or memorial of value.
- A funeral home should provide all the assistance and guidance in planning, organizing, and directing **services** that meet your needs, regardless of what casket, vault, or other merchandise you purchase.
- They should encourage family participation.
- They should be able to arrange music whether it is recorded or live.
- They should tastefully arrange pictures and memorabilia of the deceased.
- They should **assist** the clergy in planning and coordinating the memorial or funeral.
- They should explain to families all of their options, burial, cremation, or body donation, with or without services.

Most importantly, a funeral provider should assist families **after** the funeral or memorial with finalizing the details of:

- Social Security benefits
- Pension/Death Care benefits
- Veterans benefits
- Vehicle transfer of ownership
- Property transfer
- Insurance forms
- Probate court (not as a substitute for an attorney)

Many excellent funeral providers assign a staff person to assist the survivors and follow through with these details until all are complete. Other sales-oriented funeral providers just pass you off with a videotape or booklet and let you figure it out yourself.

The assistance given after the funeral or memorial is more important than the casket, vault and merchandise. Most survivors need and want help after the death of a loved one. It is worth inquiring about when considering who to choose as a provider.

How to Use This Guide

Whether you are making Pre-Need Arrangements or At Need Arrangements, an easy way to use this guide is to review and choose from the following service options:

- Body donation with no service
- Body donation with memorial services
- Cremation with no service
- Cremation with memorial service
- Cremation with funeral service
- Burial with no service. Sometimes followed by a memorial service at a later date.
- Burial with graveside service
- Burial with funeral service

1. Review just the choices that most interest you. Each choice has a corresponding section with a list of benefits, a selection of options, instructions on comparing prices, and advice on services, purchasing merchandise, and finalizing arrangements.

2. If you are considering pre-arrangements, there is a cautionary list regarding prepay and pre-need contracts.

3. There are Memorial Service Planners for information on how to plan and organize a memorial service without hiring a funeral director.

After considering all of your service options, you may find that some of the ideas put forth here will suit your needs and those of your family more than the services you have used in the past.

CREMATION AND MEMORIAL SOCIETIES
- Quick and inexpensive.
- Don't always give consumers all of their options.
- Don't explain the benefits of funerals and memorials.
- Sometimes charge as much as funeral homes for like services.

CEMETERIES WITH FUNERAL HOMES
*Limited to certain states, according to state law.
- Sometimes locally owned, sometimes corporately owned.
- Can provide complete services of traditional funeral home.
- Merchandise oriented; tend to push protective caskets, vaults, and monuments or markers.
- Not always less expensive.
- Usually regulated by the State.

PRIVATELY OWNED FUNERAL HOMES
- Locally owned.
- Usually community based and concerned.
- Not always price conscious or competitive.
- Can provide a wide range of services.
- Providers should be judged on their own skills and merits.
- Derive 50–60% of profits from sale of merchandise; tend to push "protective products."
- Regulated by State; some more strict than others.
- Tend to focus primarily on merchandise.

C O N S U M E R

CEMETERIES THAT JUST SELL MERCHANDISE
- Sometimes locally owned.
- Usually are only interested in selling merchandise, leading to high-pressure sales.
- Often don't take the time nor have the staff to provide the services of a funeral director.
- Commissioned sales people with little track record in the industry.
- Not many guarantees or safeguards if you prepay.

CORPORATE FUNERAL SERVICE
- Can own dozens to hundreds of funeral homes. Often less-than-personal service and lack of consistency between chapels.
- Sometimes they offer as many services as locally owned companies.
- Merchandise oriented; selling "protective" caskets and vaults, urns, etc. at a higher mark-up.
- Funeral Counselors may have a sales quota to meet, leading to sales pressure and higher prices.
- 50–60% of profits from sale of merchandise.
- Regulated by State.

LIFE INSURANCE COMPANY
- Publicize the cost of funerals, scaring consumers into buying more of their product.
- Many insurance policies go uncollected; many more end up costing the insured more than their actual worth.
- Proper planning eliminates these products.
- Not 100% refundable.

RETAIL CASKET STORES
- Usually locally owned.
- Try to provide merchandise to consumer at lower costs, but not always less expensive.
- Don't provide services, only merchandise.
- Get 100% of profits from merchandise.
- Not many in business longer than 10 years.
- Not many guarantees or safeguards if you prepay.

A Quick Reference for Those Who Face the Death of a Loved One

When time is at a premium, ask yourself these questions:

Q. What should I do with the deceased?
   a. Burial
   b. Cremation
   c. Body Donation

Q. What should I do with the survivors?
   a. Funeral Service (body in casket)
   b. Memorial Service (body not present)
   c. No Services

Here are some specific instructions on what to do, depending on where death occurs: PLEASE CHECK YOUR STATE LAWS.

Death occurring at a hospital:

Most hospitals have the ability to keep the deceased until the next of kin or responsible individuals can make arrangements with a funeral home, cremation society, or university for body donation. There isn't usually a charge for keeping the deceased overnight, but it is best to ask how much time you have to select a funeral home if you're undecided.

Death occurring at a nursing home:

Most nursing homes don't have facilities for keeping the deceased. Under these circumstances, the initial choice of which funeral home to use will have to be made promptly. You should be given enough time to collect needed information by telephone, whether you choose burial, cremation, or body donation.

Death occurring at home with hospice or medical care present:

If the individual has hospice or there is a medical professional on site, ask them the proper procedure for your area. Some areas have medical examiners come to the home, some physicians come to the home, and sometimes the deceased is taken to a hospital to be pronounced dead.

Unexpected death occurring at home without hospice or medical care:

Call the police and have them send an ambulance to the residence. From there the deceased is taken to the hospital to be pronounced dead. In some areas, medical examiners will come to the home to pronounce the person dead.

Death occurring away from home— Vacation, Business, etc:

The deceased is usually taken to the nearest hospital to be pronounced dead. If you decide to send the deceased home for burial, call funeral homes in the town where death occurred for price information and assistance in getting the deceased home. Almost always the receiving funeral home can obtain better pricing on the services of removal, embalming and transportation. If you decide to have cremation, you can contact the providers in the area where death occurred, and eliminate the extra charges involved with shipping the deceased. You do not have to purchase a casket for shipping by air, or by hearse.

The following are 8 possible options from which you can choose.

- Body donation with no services
- Body donation with a memorial service
- Cremation with no services
- Cremation with a memorial service, the body not present.
- Cremation with a funeral (services at a funeral home or church), the body would be in a casket, services conclude there.
- Burial with no services. Sometimes followed by a memorial service at a later date.
- Burial with graveside services at the cemetery.
- Burial with a funeral, services at a funeral home or church

Each of the above options is covered in this book. Use the enclosed forms to compare service and merchandise prices.

PART 2

Service Options

Body Donation—No Service

STEP 1   Read the pros and cons of Body Donation with No Service

STEP 2   Determine if these arrangements meet the approval of survivors

STEP 3   Choose options

STEP 4   Gather price information

STEP 5   Compare prices, services, and attitudes of providers

STEP 6   Finalize arrangements

STEP 7   The careful approach

STEP 1

Pros

- Provides vital educational resources.

- Low cost.

- Saves land.

- Eliminates costs associated with cremation and burial: caskets, vaults, urns, embalming, and cemetery or crematory fees.

- Prices are easily compared.

Cons

NOTE—Medical schools and other accepting facilities have requirements regarding the physical condition of the deceased. It is strongly recommended that you contact the accepting facility in your area prior to the need and inquire about their procedures and requirements. (See page 28, Gift of Human Anatomy) Ordinarily, they will provide a donor card for you to carry and will keep a copy of your wishes on file. See sections in this book on Cremation or Burial if your donation is denied acceptance at a university or institution.

- Most, not all, institutions do not want the body embalmed by the funeral home.

- Anyone wanting to view the deceased would have to do so either at the place of death (i.e. hospital, nursing home) or in the funeral home's preparation room, before the deceased is taken to the accepting institution.

- Institutions can refuse acceptance if, at the time of death, the deceased is in such a physical condition that they cannot be used for medical study.

- The cost of transportation to the medical facility may be more than a simple cremation.

- In some states you may be charged for arterial embalming.

STEP 2

Approval of Survivors

- In a pre-need situation, determine if the arrangements you are making meet the approval of your next of kin or survivors. In some states, pre-need arrangements can be changed by survivors after death has occurred. However, arrangements need not be altered if they are discussed and survivors understand your wishes while you are living.

STEP 3

Choose options

- Various services offered by the funeral home
- Obituary
- Memorial Announcement

Funeral Home Services

- The death of a family member, friend, or loved one will find you in no mood to make multitudes of difficult decisions. If you are responsible for making someone's funeral or memorial services, then pre-thinking and pre-planning your options—not pre-paying—is helpful.

- In Step 5, you will shop for the "best price" and the "best services." It will be difficult to put a dollar value on the compassion and care given to your family, so it is important to take a minute to think about your own situation and the assistance they will need.

- In addition to the basic services that all funeral homes offer, there are "additional" services made available by **some** funeral homes. In many cases, these services are the most appreciated functions a funeral home offers because they can make your family's burden more bearable.

- Assistance with Death Certificates: It will be necessary to notify various business and governmental agencies that death has occurred. The following list will help you decide how much assistance you may need to complete these tasks. Many funeral homes offer services for this and can be of invaluable assistance.

  > Real estate transfers

  > Probate court

  > Motor vehicles (cars, trucks, boats, etc.)

  > Banks, brokers, investments

  > Veterans' affairs: 1-800-827-1000

  > Social security

  > Life insurance

  > Pension benefits

- **Some** funeral homes schedule a meeting with the family, providing clerical assistance and transportation to the above offices and agencies. If you need this service, inquire about the price and decide if the cost is worth the trouble it will save you and your survivors.

- Survivors Workshops: The funeral director should be able to direct you to a group which assists survivors of suicide, sudden infant death, AIDS, etc. Hospitals, church groups, and non-profit organizations often sponsor these activities.

Obituary

- Your primary option is to have an obituary notice, possibly naming an organization where memorial contributions may be sent. This will allow family and friends to express their sympathy in lieu of memorial services or a funeral (see page 147).

Memorial Announcement

- A memorial announcement can be an appropriate, effective, and inexpensive method to notify a selective group of people that someone has died. Memorial announcements can be personalized to meet any family's needs. It can be very effective for notifying friends and family who live far away. *Take this book with you to a PRINTER and show them exactly what you want, using the enclosed samples of memorial announcements (see page 149).*

STEP 4

Gather Price Information

NOTE—If you don't ask, you could be comparing prices from the same firm, which could lead you to believe that prices must be consistent across the board.

- Using the Telephone Checklist on the next page and the Yellow Page section of your phone book, call at least three funeral homes for price information. When calling, ask each funeral home if they are associated with or co-owned by any other funeral homes in your area. It is common for a conglomerate to own several funeral homes and cemeteries in an area and operate under different names.

- It is required by law in all 50 states that price information be given over the phone.

- Surveys have shown that prices can range considerably in areas with little competition. Don't be hesitant to call for prices in neighboring communities. The savings may be well worth the call, especially if you're not holding services.

- If you prefer, visit the funeral homes of choice and request a **General Price List**. *It is required by law that upon request, General Price Lists be given to the public.*

Telephone Checklist

NOTE: It is very important to obtain accurate prices for the services you desire, so request totals. Bait and switch discrepancies may arise during final arrangements if you don't obtain exact price quotes in the beginning.

I am calling for "package" price information on a Body Donation to

_____ without a memorial service.

(name of facility or university)

	Company Example*	Company A	Company B	Company C
Funeral Home Name:	Sunset			
Funeral Home Representative:	John Doe			
Date:	9/01/02			
Phone Number:	810-230-0000			
	PRICES	PRICES	PRICES	PRICES
**Packaged Services for Body Donation	$600*			
Transportation to Facility:	$100*			
Other Services:	None chosen			
TOTAL:	$700*			

* The prices above are meant to be merely examples

** Itemized prices may be more expensive.

Additional Expenses—Not Necessary to Compare—Obtain Prices only for Planning Final Cost

Additional Expenses	Example	Price
Option of Obituary	$100*	
Memorial Announcement	$25*	
Number of Death Certificates (5)	$30*	
Other		
TOTAL ADDITIONAL EXPENSES:	$155*	
Total from above:	$700*	
TOTAL SERVICES, MERCHANDISE, AND ADDITIONAL EXPENSES:	$855*	

* The prices above are meant to be merely examples

These expenses will primarily be the same for all funeral homes, but knowing their prices will help determine total costs. If these expenses are added into your contract, you may be paying an extra fee, or the funeral home may receive a discount for completing these services.

STEP 5

**Compare Prices
and Services**

- Compare funeral homes' prices and their willingness to assist you. Since you will not be using their facilities for viewing or services, it is not necessary to visit them to compare these prices or services prior to finalizing arrangements.

- It is required by law that General Price Lists be given to the public upon request.

STEP 6

Finalize Arrangements

NOTE—Compare their General Price List with the prices given over the phone. Do this prior to any conversation regarding services or merchandise. If there are any differences or you are not satisfied, request an explanation. If you are still not satisfied, leave. It may be necessary to report them to the Federal Trade Commission. Funeral homes are responsible for all employees who quote prices, and can be held accountable.

- Make an appointment to meet with the funeral home of your choice. Take this guide along with the following:

  > Completed obituary form (page 147)—optional

  > Completed death certificate form (page 151)

  > Memorial announcement information (page 149)—optional

- Final arrangements should be written so that anyone can read and clearly understand the exact services or merchandise purchased.

STEP 7

The Careful Approach

- If you decide to prepay your services, be sure you understand all arrangements and have them in writing.

- Ask any of the following questions that you feel are necessary:

  > Is my money 100 percent refundable at any time?

  > Can I transfer my arrangements without penalty?

  > Where will my money be placed (bank, savings & loan, insurance, or trust)?

> Will I receive a receipt and proof of deposit after payment?

> What is your commission?

> What written guarantees do I have that my funds are available when needed?

> Is my account insured? If yes, by whom?

> Will I pay taxes on my earned interest?

> If your funeral home is sold, can I obtain or transfer my money without penalty?

> Is my money sheltered if I have to go on Medicaid?

> If you go out of business, what happens to my money?

> Are you licensed by the state? If yes, please provide proof, including your insurance identification number.

> If I cancel my arrangements several years from now, who keeps the earned interest?

- If the above questions are not answered to your satisfaction, **do not pay**. If the answers given are not in writing, **do not pay**. If you are pressured, **do not pay**. If you have not compared at least three firms, **do not pay**.

Gift of Human Anatomy to the University

Pursuant to the provisions of the Uniform Anatomical Gift Act, Article 10 of the Michigan Public Health Code, I hereby give my whole body, to be delivered after my death as provided in the aforementioned law, to the Department of Anatomy and Cell Biology of the University Medical School to be used in medical education, teaching, and research. To fulfill the purposes hereby intended, my body is not to be autopsied nor are parts to be removed for transplant without first contacting the Anatomical Donations Office.

I have checked those statements below that apply to my intended donation:

_____ My body may be used in any manner that the University Medical School deems necessary.

_____ My body may be utilized for teaching and research at the University Medical School only.

_____ My body may be utilized for teaching and research at an institution other than the University Medical School.

_____ Organs or parts of my body (other than the whole body) may be used for teaching and research at the University Medical School.

_____ Organs or parts of my body may be used for teaching and research at any institution other than the University Medical School.

_____ Organs or parts of my body may be permanently preserved for teaching purposes at the University Medical School.

_____ I am registered with an organ/tissue donation agency.

Has a relative donated before? _____ Yes   _____ No

Name of relative:_____

Complete and sign this form and keep the second copy for your records.

(Space for your name, address, date of birth, telephone number, signature, and signature of two witnesses will also be provided on the form from the University or facility you choose.)

This form is to be used as a sample ONLY. You may wish to check with the University to which you wish to make the donation to see if they utilize any particular form.

Body Donation—With Memorial Service

STEP 1   Read the pros and cons of Body Donations with Memorial Service

STEP 2   Determine if these arrangements meet the approval of survivors

STEP 3   Choose options

STEP 4   Detailed description of options

STEP 5   Gather price information

STEP 6   Compare prices, services, and attitudes of providers

STEP 7   Finalize arrangements

STEP 8   The careful approach

STEP 1

Pros

- Provides vital educational resources.

- Low cost.

- Saves land.

- Eliminates costs associated with cremation and burial: caskets, vaults, urns, embalming, and cemetery or crematory fees.

- Prices are easily compared.

- You do not have to hire a funeral home to plan or conduct a memorial service (see page 45).

- Provides the same elements valued in funeral services, without having the body present:

    > Allows flexible time scheduling (days, weeks, months) after one dies.

    > Simple to plan.

    > Does not require professional assistance (although it may be helpful in some cases).

    > Provides closure—a sense of finality.

    > Can be as simple or elaborate as one chooses.

    > Can include the use of many options such as music, flowers, photographs, and alternative site selection.

Cons

NOTE—Medical schools and other accepting facilities have requirements regarding the physical condition of the deceased. It is strongly recommended that you contact the accepting facility in your area prior to the need and inquire about their procedures and requirements. (See page 44, Gift of Human Anatomy) Ordinarily, they will provide a donor card for you to carry and will keep a copy of your wishes on file. See sections in this book on Cremation or Burial with Memorial Service if your donation is denied acceptance at a university or institution.

- Most, not all, institutions do not want the body embalmed by the funeral home, thus making prolonged viewing impossible.

- Anyone wanting to view the deceased would have to do so either at the place of death (i.e. hospital, nursing home) or at the funeral home, before the deceased is taken to the accepting institution.

- Institutions can refuse acceptance if, at the time of death, the deceased is in such a physical condition that they cannot be used for medical study.

- Cost of transportation to the medical facility may be more than a simlple cremation.

- In some states you may be charged for arterial embalming.

STEP 2

Approval of Survivors

- In a pre-need situation, determine if the arrangements you are making meet the approval of your next of kin or survivors. In some states, survivors can change pre-arrangements after death has occurred. However, arrangements need not be altered if they are discussed and survivors understand your wishes while you are living.

- Planning a memorial service requires making phone calls and coordinating the efforts of a few people.

- You should consider your survivors' abilities to organize and conduct the memorial service without the aid of a funeral director. In Step 4 and on page 46, there is a list with explanations of each option they will face while planning a memorial service. People plan their own weddings; why not memorial services?

- While gathering price information, consider the cost of hiring a funeral director. Read Step 4: Detailed Description of Options, while planning a memorial service.

STEP 3

Choose Options

- While reviewing the following options and making decisions regarding memorial services, determine if YOU want to organize the memorial service or hire a funeral director. Even if you hire a funeral director, many of the responsibilities and decisions will still be yours.

- When calling funeral homes for price information, ask for prices *with* and *without* their services for arranging and conducting memorial services. If you decide to plan and organize your own memorial service, see the following pages for help with the details:

    > Various services offered by the funeral home

    > Date and time of memorial service

    > Location of memorial service

    > Use of clergy or speaker

    > Number of people attending

> Music

> Private or public service

> Memorial accessories:
>> —memorial folders
>> —prayer cards
>> —register book
>> —thank-you notes

> Memorial announcement

> Obituary

> Greeters and ushers

> Flowers and choice of florist

> Luncheon following memorial service

> Pictures and memorabilia

> Visitation times before memorial service

> Military services

> Fraternal orders

STEP 4

Detailed Description of Options

Funeral Home Services

- The death of a family member, friend, or loved one will find you in no mood to make multitudes of difficult decisions. If you are responsible for making someone's funeral or memorial services, then pre-thinking and pre-planning your options—not pre-paying—is helpful.

- In Step 5, you will shop for the "best price" and the "best services." It will be difficult to put a dollar value on the compassion and care given to your family, so it is important to take a minute to think about your own situation and the assistance they will need before, during, and after the service.

- In addition to the basic services that all funeral homes offer, there are "additional" services made available by **some** funeral homes. In many cases, these services are the most appreciated functions a funeral home offers because they can make your family's burden more bearable.

- Assistance with Death Certificates: It will be necessary to notify various business and governmental agencies that death has occurred. The following list will help you decide how much assistance you may need to complete these tasks. Many funeral homes offer services for this and can be of invaluable assistance.

  > Real estate transfers

  > Probate court

  > Motor vehicles (cars, trucks, boats, etc.)

  > Banks, brokers, investments

  > Veterans affairs

  > Social security

  > Life insurance

  > Pension benefits

- **Some** funeral homes schedule a meeting with the family, providing clerical assistance and transportation to the above offices and agencies. If you need this service, inquire about the price and decide if the cost is worth the trouble it will save you and your survivors.

- Flower Delivery: Sometimes it is difficult to load all plants, flowers, etc., into your vehicles. Some funeral homes provide this in their professional services fees, while others will charge a separate fee.

- Meals: After the memorial service, the funeral director should be able to reserve or recommend a place that accommodates memorial luncheons.

- Hotel Accommodations: The funeral director should be able to recommend a nearby place that is within your budget and suitable to your needs.

- Survivors Workshops: The funeral director should be able to direct you to a group which assists survivors of suicide, sudden infant death, AIDS, etc. Hospitals, church groups, and non-profit organizations often sponsor these activities.

Date and Time

- Before you set a date and time, make sure all facilities, people involved (family from out of town), clergy, luncheon facility, flower shop, etc. can accommodate or attend on that date and at that time. A few quick phone calls can prevent having to change plans at the last minute.

Location of Memorial Services

- Churches and funeral homes are common locations for memorial services. However, memorial services can be held anywhere people can gather, considering seating capacity, parking, time of year, and availability.

- Alternative locations for memorial services:

  > Fraternal halls (e.g. Eagles, Moose, Elks)

  > Masonic Temple, Knights of Columbus Hall

  > Parks

  > Residence

  > Ocean side/lakeside

  > Favorite saloon

  > Golf course

  > University

- *Even if you are not a member, many churches will allow you to use their facility for a reasonable fee*—usually for much less than the cost of using a funeral home's facilities. Many churches have sound systems, plenty of seating, parking, and a place for a luncheon following the services.

Clergy or Speaker

- Consider what you want to be said and the desired formality of services **before** choosing your speaker or clergy. **Before** planning too far, check that the person is available. It is very important to give them a few written ideas of what you want to be said and the music to be played. It is highly recommended that you meet this person and make sure that they have a clear understanding of your expectations. If you want an upbeat, uplifting memorial with special music, say so.

Number of People

- Factors that determine the number of people attending a memorial service could be the age of the deceased, social and church involvement, achievements, and whether or not an obituary was placed in the paper. The reasons for needing to know approximately how many people will attend:

  > Number of memorial folders (optional)

  > Size and location of facility to be used

  > Number of people for luncheon (optional)

  > Assistance needed at memorial service

Music

- Music is often the most overlooked and under-utilized aspect of a memorial service. It can be very comforting and uplifting to use music in conjunction with the spoken message. By using "personal favorite" selections, whether they are traditional hymns, modern music, contemporary, jazz, country, rock, or spiritual, you will be adding beauty and meaning to the service. With some planning, such accompaniments as piano, violin, bagpipes, guitar, flute, or a soloist singing a favorite song can add a great deal to services that have traditionally been limited to traditional hymns.

- Some creative and memorable musical selections requested by families for memorial services have been: "Take Me Out To The Ball Game"; "My Way," by Frank Sinatra; "Somewhere Over The Rainbow," by Judy Garland; "Danny Boy," by Kate Smith; "Stairway To Heaven," by Led Zeppelin (used for a teenager killed in an auto accident); "Amazing Grace" (played on bagpipes); "Unforgettable," by Nat King Cole; "Evergreen," by Barbara Streisand; "Ave Maria," by Pavarotti; "Bridge Over Troubled Water," by Simon and Garfunkel; "Desperado," by The Eagles and "The National Anthem," by Arthur Fiedler and the Boston Philharmonic (Veterans Service).

- Most churches and funeral homes have the necessary sound equipment to play cassettes or compact discs, and given enough time, can arrange for musicians. If you are having services at an "alternative" site and would like a musician, call a church, college/ university or an institute of music for a referral.

Private or Public Memorial Services

- Sometimes immediate friends and families can be more comforting than hoards of people you may not know, or may not care to see at that time. If you opt for a private memorial service, mention it in the obituary or do not run an obituary until after the service is held.

Memorial Accessories

- Memorial Folders: Memorial folders are traditionally used for Protestant services, and are available through funeral homes, some church supply stores, and printers. Their purpose is debatable, since most end up left on church pews or folded up in a pocket, later to be discarded.

- Prayer Cards: Prayer cards are traditionally used for Catholic and Orthodox faiths and are available through funeral homes, some church supply stores, and printers.

- Register Books: Register books are especially helpful if they have name and address lines to aid in sending "thank-you" notes, if so desired. Register books are frequently sold at funeral homes for $25.00 to $65.00, and similar products are available for much less through stationary and church supply stores.

- Thank-you Notes: Thank-you notes are usually sent to those that pay a special kindness to you such as sending flowers, making memorial contributions to charitable organizations, assisting in memorial services, and providing food for a luncheon. They are available at funeral homes, stationary stores, and card shops. It is usually worth shopping around; sometimes selections offered at funeral homes are limited and expensive.

Memorial Announcement

- Using a memorial announcement can be an appropriate, effective, and inexpensive method of notifying a selective group of people that someone has died. Memorial announcements can be personalized to meet a family's needs. It can be very effective for notifying friends and family who live far away. **Take this book with you to a PRINTER and show them exactly what you want from the Memorial Announcement samples on page 149.**

Obituaries

- These can include a wide variety of information useful in notifying friends, family, and business associates. They are especially helpful when they include specific information about visitation times, location, date, time of services, and a listing of charitable organizations where contributions may be sent (see page 147).

Greeters/Ushers

- Greeters and ushers can be members of the family or close friends who are willing to help greet people, hang coats, ask visitors to sign the register book, and hand out memorial folders or prayer cards.

Florist

- Similar to music, flowers are one of the most overlooked options of a memorial service. Many florists simply do not have experience or talent advising families about the use of flowers in conjunction with memorial services. When meeting with the florist, consider the following: Pictures, memorabilia, size of facility, and flower stands available through the florist or the funeral home. By using a competent florist who is interested in working with the aforementioned elements, flowers can add beauty and warmth to the memorial service.

Luncheon

- Serving lunch after a memorial service is sometimes quite nice, whether you serve coffee and pastry or a multi-course meal provided by a top-notch restaurant or caterer. Luncheons offer a chance for friends to talk and families to come together, which may begin the process of healing.

Use of Pictures, Videos, or Memorabilia

• Pictures taken throughout a person's life can be very important and meaningful in terms of comforting a family. You can use pictures, photographs, and videos to remember a person when they were happy, successful, content, in love, proud; the list is endless. Such pictures can be more meaningful than viewing a body which, due to injury or illness, is not what you care to remember.

Visitation

• Consider allowing a period of time before or after the service to visit with friends and family. If you are having an obituary printed, it is suggested that such times be listed.

Military Services

• If a person served during a time of war and was honorably discharged from the military, he or she should be entitled to military services. The local Veterans of Foreign Wars organization (V.F.W.) can usually arrange for a graveside service including a chaplain, bugler, honor guard, and gun salute.

Fraternal/Religious Organization Services

• There are too many to list, but if a person had a strong affiliation with such organizations as the Masons, Demolay, or Knights of Columbus, they will quite often have a memorial service at the funeral home the evening before the funeral service if you so choose.

STEP 5

Gather Price Information

NOTE—If you don't ask, you could be comparing prices from the same firm, which could lead you to believe that prices must be consistent across the board.

- Using the Telephone Checklist on the next page and the Yellow Page section of your phone book, call at least three funeral homes for price information. When calling, ask each funeral home if they are associated with or co-owned by any other funeral homes in your area. It is common for a conglomerate to own several funeral homes and cemeteries in an area and operate under different names.

- It is required by law in all 50 states that price information be given over the phone.

- Surveys have shown that prices can range considerably in areas with little competition. Don't be hesitant to call for prices in neighboring communities. The savings may be well worth the call.

- If you prefer, visit the funeral homes of choice and request a **General Price List**. *It is required by law that upon request, General Price Lists be given to the public.*

Telephone Checklist

NOTE: It is very important to obtain accurate prices for the services you desire, so request totals. Bait and switch discrepancies may arise during final arrangements if you don't obtain exact price quotes in the beginning.

I am calling for price information on a Body Donation to

_____

(name of facility or university)

with a memorial service held at

_____

(name of funeral home or church)

	Company Example	Company A	Company B	Company C
Funeral Home Name:	Sunset			
Funeral Home Representative:	John Doe			
Date:	9/01/02			
Phone Number:	810-230-0000			
	PRICES	PRICES	PRICES	PRICES
Basic Services of Funeral Director & Staff:	$500*			
Conducting Memorial Service—Optional:	$300*			
Private Family Viewing:	$0*			
Use of Funeral Home for Memorial—Optional:	$200*			
Removal from Place of Death:	$100*			
Transportation to Facility:	$100*			
Register Book:	$25*			
Service Folders/Prayer Cards:	$25*			
Thank-you Notes:	$15*			
Other:				
TOTAL:	$1,265*			
Total Without Use of Funeral Home for Memorial:	$1,065*			
Total Without Use of Funeral Director and Funeral Home for Memorial:	$765*			

* The prices above are meant to be merely examples

Additional Expenses—Not Necessary to Compare—Obtain Prices only for Planning Final Cost

Additional Expenses	Example	Price
Option of Obituary	$100*	
Number of Death Certificates (5)	$30*	
Musicians/organist/soloist	$100*	
Clergy	$100*	
Church Fees:	No Charge*	
Luncheon:	$250*	
Memorial Announcement:	$25*	
Florist:	$200*	
Other:	None*	
TOTAL ADDITIONAL EXPENSES:	$805*	

* The prices above are meant to be merely examples

These expenses will primarily be the same for all funeral homes, but knowing their prices will help determine total costs. If these expenses are added into your contract, you may be paying an extra fee, or the funeral home may receive a discount for completing these services.

STEP 6

Compare Prices

- Compare funeral homes' prices and their willingness to serve you.

- How willing is a funeral home to tailor services that meet your needs. Funeral directors will bend over backwards if they can take a consumer away from a competitor.

- Inspect facilities for cleanliness, adequate parking, and handicap accessibility. Ask to see the area where your service will be held and ask about their ability to assist you with music selections or other options you have chosen.

STEP 7

Finalize Arrangements and Services

NOTE—Final arrangements should be written so that anyone can read and clearly understand the exact services or merchandise purchased. Compare their General Price List with the prices given over the phone. Do this prior to any conversation regarding services or merchandise. If there are any differences or if you are not satisfied, request an explanation. If you are still not satisfied, leave. It may be necessary to report them to the Federal Trade Commission. Funeral Homes are responsible for all employees who quote prices, and can be held accountable.

- Make an appointment to meet with the funeral home of your choice. Take this guide along with the following:

  > Completed obituary form (page 147)—optional

  > Completed death certificate form (page 151)

  > List of options you will use (see Step 3).

  > If you need assistance locating clergy, a soloist, or if you have questions regarding death certificates, now is the time to inquire.

STEP 8

The Careful Approach

- *If you decide to prepay your services, be sure you understand all arrangements and have them in writing.*

- Ask any of the following questions that you feel are necessary:

  > Is my money 100 percent refundable at any time?

  > Can I transfer my arrangements without penalty?

  > Where will my money be placed (bank, savings & loan, insurance, or trust)?

  > Will I receive a receipt and proof of deposit after payment?

  > What is your commission?

  > What written guarantees do I have that my funds are available when needed?

  > Is my account insured? If yes, by whom?

  > Will I pay taxes on my earned interest?

  > If your funeral home is sold, can I obtain or transfer my money without penalty?

  > Is my money sheltered if I have to go on Medicaid?

  > If you go out of business, what happens to my money?

  > Are you licensed by the state? If yes, please provide proof, including your insurance identification number.

  > If I cancel my arrangements several years from now, who keeps the earned interest?

- If the above questions are not answered to your satisfaction, **do not pay.** If the answers given are not in writing, **do not pay.** If you are pressured, **do not pay.** If you have not compared at least three firms, **do not pay.**

SAMPLE FORM

Gift of Human Anatomy to the University

Pursuant to the provisions of the Uniform Anatomical Gift Act, Article 10 of the Michigan Public Health Code, I hereby give my whole body, to be delivered after my death as provided in the aforementioned law, to the Department of Anatomy and Cell Biology of the University Medical School to be used in medical education, teaching, and research. To fulfill the purposes hereby intended, my body is not to be autopsied nor are parts to be removed for transplant without first contacting the Anatomical Donations Office.

I have checked those statements below that apply to my intended donation:

_____ My body may be used in any manner that the University Medical School deems necessary.

_____ My body may be utilized for teaching and research at the University Medical School only.

_____ My body may be utilized for teaching and research at an institution other than the University Medical School.

_____ Organs or parts of my body (other than the whole body) may be used for teaching and research at the University Medical School.

_____ Organs or parts of my body may be used for teaching and research at any institution other than the University Medical School.

_____ Organs or parts of my body may be permanently preserved for teaching purposes at the University Medical School.

_____ I am registered with an organ/tissue donation agency.

Has a relative donated before? _____ Yes   _____ No

Name of relative:_____

Complete and sign this form and keep the second copy for your records.

(Space for your name, address, date of birth, telephone number, signature, and signature of two witnesses will also be provided on the form from the University or facility you choose.)

This form is to be used as a sample ONLY. You may wish to check with the University to which you wish to make the donation to see if they utilize any particular gift forms.

EXAMPLE—Memorial Service Planner

This planner is to be utilized for planning memorial services, in lieu of hiring a funeral director.

	ARRANGEMENT DETAILS	ARRANGED OR CONFIRMED BY	PAYMENT
Time/Date	1:00 p.m. Wednesday, August 26	Confirmed by Church Secretary	Not Applicable
Place	First United Methodist Church	Rev. Jones	No Charge for church members
Church Phone #	(612) 659-1000	Parish Office	Not Applicable
Clergy/Speaker	Reverend Jones	Rev. Jones	$100.00—PAID*
Meeting w/family	5:00 p.m., Tuesday, August 25	Rev. Jones	Not Applicable
Music	Piano music before/after services	Church music dir.	$50.00—PAID*
Soloist	Mr. Graham from church	Mr. Graham	$50.00—PAID*
Special Songs/Tape	"Amazing Grace", "Danny Boy"	Music Dir. has music	Not Applicable
Register Book	Sunset Funeral Home	Purchased at Sunset Funeral Home	$25.00—PAID*
Memorial Programs	Handled by Sunset Funeral Home	Sunset Funeral Home	$25.00—PAID*
Thank you notes	Purchased at funeral home	Sunset Funeral Home	$15.00—PAID*
Obituary	One day, local paper	Placed in paper by Sunset Funeral Home	$100.00—PAID*
Visitation Times	Noon–1:00 p.m., August 26	Times confirmed by church secretary	Not Applicable
Veteran Services	Not a Veteran	Not a Veteran	Not Applicable
Flag	None	Not chosen	Not Applicable
Masonic or Knights of Columbus	Not a member	Not a member	Not Applicable
Florist	Elegant Florist	Ordered from Larry, August 24	$200.00—PAID*
Luncheon	Following memorial at church social hall	Church secretary confirmed	Included in payment to church*
Caterer	Complete catering (50–75 people)	Mr. Young confirmed	$250.00—PAID*
Church Setup	Pictures and memorabilia on communion table		
Greeters/Ushers	Uncle Ed and Uncle Harold	Aunt Charlene	No Charge*
Memorial Announcement	Ordered through Kinko's Printers	Mr. O'Leary at Kinko's Printers	$25.00—PAID*
Miscellaneous	Make room reservations for out-of-town family members (20 people)	Made reservations for 20 people	Paid by individual family members*

* The prices above are meant to be merely examples

Memorial Service Planner

This planner is to be utilized for planning memorial services, in lieu of hiring a funeral director.

	ARRANGEMENT DETAILS	ARRANGED/CONFIRMED BY	PAYMENT
TIME/DATE			
PLACE			
CHURCH PHONE #			
CLERGY/SPEAKER			
MEETING W/FAMILY			
MUSIC			
SOLOIST			
SPECIAL SONGS/TAPE			
REGISTER BOOK			
MEMORIAL PROGRAMS			
THANK-YOU NOTES			
OBITUARY			
VISITATION TIMES			
VETERAN SERVICES			
FLAG			
MASONIC / KNIGHTS OF COLUMBUS			
FLORIST			
LUNCHEON			
CATERER			
CHURCH SETUP			
GREETERS/ USHERS			
MEMORIAL ANNOUNCEMENT			
MISCELLANEOUS			

Cremation—No Service

STEP 1   Read the pros and cons of Cremation with No Service

STEP 2   Determine if these arrangements meet the approval of survivors

STEP 3   Choose options

STEP 4   Gather price information

STEP 5   Compare prices, services, and attitudes of providers

STEP 6   Finalize arrangements

STEP 7   The careful approach

STEP 1

Pros	

Pros

- Low cost. Purchase of an urn is optional.

- Saves land.

- Eliminates costs associated with burial: caskets, vaults, embalming, and cemetery services of opening and closing a grave.

- Prices are easily compared.

- Able to use an "alternative container" instead of a casket for cremation.

Cons

NOTE—In most states, the next of kin will be required to sign a "Cremation Authorization Form" provided by the funeral home, crematory, or both.

WARNING—Sometimes funeral directors or cremation society operators insist that a family identify the body before cremation and will attempt to sell the family an expensive container in which to view the deceased. If this occurs, request that the identification be made on their dressing table.

- Limits viewing the deceased. Anyone wanting to view the deceased would have to do so either at the place of death (i.e., hospital, nursing home) or at the funeral home's preparation facility, before the deceased is taken to the crematory.

- There may be a charge for private family viewing without embalming if they dress the body and set the features of the deceased.

- Some funeral homes limit the time permitted. Ask for an hourly rate if so desired.

STEP 2

Approval of Survivors

- In a pre-need situation, determine if the arrangements you are making meet the approval of your next of kin or survivors. In some states, survivors can change pre-arrangements after death has occurred. However, arrangements need not be altered if they are discussed and survivors understand your wishes while you are living.

STEP 3

Choose Options

- Various services offered by the funeral home
- Obituary
- Memorial Announcement
- Disposition of ashes
- Urns

Funeral Home Services

- The death of a family member, friend, or loved one will find you in no mood to make multitudes of difficult decisions. If you are responsible for making someone's funeral or memorial services, then thinking and pre-planning your options—not pre-paying—is helpful.

- In Step 5, you will shop for the "best price" and the "best services." It will be difficult to put a dollar value on the compassion and care given to your family, so it is important to take a minute to think about your own situation and the assistance they will need before, during, and after the cremation.

- In addition to the basic services that all funeral homes offer, there are "additional" services made available by **some** funeral homes. In many cases, these services are the most appreciated functions a funeral home offers because they can make your family's burden more bearable.

- Assistance with Death Certificates: It will be necessary to notify various business and governmental agencies that death has occurred. The following list will help you decide how much assistance you may need to complete these tasks. Many funeral homes offer services for this and can be of invaluable assistance.

    > Real estate transfers

    > Probate court

    > Motor vehicles (cars, trucks, boats, etc.)

    > Banks, brokers, investments

    > Veterans affairs: 1-800-827-1000

    > Social security

    > Life insurance

    > Pension benefits

- **Some** funeral homes schedule a meeting with the family, providing clerical assistance and transportation to the above offices and agencies. If you need this service, inquire about the price and decide if the cost is worth the trouble it will save you and your survivors.

- Survivors Workshops: The funeral director should be able to direct you to a group which assists survivors of suicide, sudden infant death, AIDS, etc. Hospitals, church groups, and non-profit organizations often sponsor these activities.

Obituary

- Your primary option is to have an obituary notice, possibly naming an organization where memorial contributions may be sent. This will allow family and friends to express their sympathy in lieu of memorial services or a funeral (see page 147).

Memorial Announcement

- A memorial announcement can be an appropriate, effective, and inexpensive method to notify a selective group of people that someone has died. Memorial announcements can be personalized to meet a family's needs. It can be very effective for notifying friends and family who live far away. *Take this book with you to a PRINTER and show them exactly what you want, using the enclosed samples of memorial announcements in this guide (see page 149).*

Disposition of Ashes

- Your options for disposition of ashes include, but are not limited to:
    - > Scattering
    - > Placing ashes in a Columbarium or Mausoleum niche
    - > Burial in a cemetery. If you own cemetery property, check to see about its regulations and fees.

Urns

- There are very few requirements made to account for a family's disposition of ashes. Some states have laws that forbid scattering on public lands. Before purchasing an urn, consider what you will be doing with the ashes. It is not necessary or required by law to purchase an urn for any method of disposition. Urns are mostly used for display, at home or in a niche at a Columbarium. If a crematory or funeral home insists that you purchase an urn, you may provide your own container or vase, probably for much less money than the cost of those offered.

- Most crematories place the ashes in a plastic bag and then into a hard plastic box before giving them to the family or funeral director. *This container is suitable for burial and for holding the ashes until scattering is complete.*

STEP 4

Gather Price Information

NOTE—If you don't ask, you could be comparing prices from the same firm, which could lead you to believe that prices must be consistent across the board.

- Using the Telephone Checklist on the next page and the Yellow Page section of your phone book, call at least three funeral homes for price information. When calling, ask each funeral home if they are associated with or co-owned by any other funeral homes in your area. It is common for a conglomerate to own several funeral homes and cemeteries in an area and operate under different names.

- It is required by law in all 50 states that price information be given over the phone.

- Surveys have shown that prices can range considerably in areas with little competition. Don't be hesitant to call for prices in neighboring communities. The savings may be well worth the call.

- If you prefer, visit the funeral homes of choice and request a **General Price List**. *It is required by law that upon request, General Price Lists be given to the public.*

Telephone Checklist

NOTE: It is very important to obtain accurate prices for the services you desire, so request totals. Bait and switch discrepancies may arise during final arrangements if you don't obtain exact price quotes in the beginning.

I am calling for package price information for direct cremation including the alternative minimum container and cost of cremation (sometimes called immediate cremation).

	Company Example	Company A	Company B	Company C
Funeral Home Name:	Sunset			
Funeral Home Representative:	John Doe			
Date:	9/01/02			
Phone Number:	810-230-0000			
	PRICES	PRICES	PRICES	PRICES
Package Price for Direct Cremation, Alternative Minimum Container and Crematory Fee:	$750*			
Urn—Optional:	$100*			
Other Services:	None chosen*			
TOTAL:	$850*			

* The prices above are meant to be merely examples
** Package prices are usually less than itemized.

Additional Expenses—Not Necessary to Compare—Obtain Prices only for Planning Final Cost

Additional Expenses	Example	Price
Crematory (if not included above)	$0*	
Obituary	$100*	
Memorial Announcement	$25*	
Number of Death Certificates (5)	$30*	
Other		
TOTAL ADDITIONAL EXPENSES:	$155*	
Total from above:	$850*	
TOTAL SERVICES, MERCHANDISE, AND ADDITIONAL EXPENSES:	$1,005*	

* The prices above are meant to be merely examples

These expenses will primarily be the same for all funeral homes, but knowing their prices will help determine total costs. If these expenses are added into your contract, you may be paying an extra fee, or the funeral home may receive a discount for completing these services.

STEP 5

Compare Prices and Services

Remember that you do not have to purchase all merchandise or services from the same business. If you decide to have the cremation handled by one funeral home and purchase the urn elsewhere, that is perfectly all right. You cannot be penalized or charged more.

- Compare funeral homes' prices to crematory prices (in states which allow a crematory to conduct such services) and their willingness to assist you.

- How willing is a funeral home to tailor services that meet your needs? If they are not willing, choose another. Funeral directors will bend over backwards if they can take a consumer away from a competitor.

- It is required by law that General Price Lists be given to the public upon request.

STEP 6

Finalize Arrangements

NOTE—Compare their General Price List with the prices given over the phone. Do this prior to any conversation regarding services or merchandise. If there are any differences or if you are not satisfied, request an explanation. If you are still not satisfied, leave. It may be necessary to report them to the Federal Trade Commission. Funeral Homes are responsible for all employees who quote prices, and can be held accountable.

- Make an appointment to meet with the funeral home or crematory (where states allow) of your choice. Take this guide along with the following:

  > Completed obituary form (page 147)—optional

  > Completed death certificate form (page 151)

  > Finalized decision on disposition of ashes

- Final arrangements should be written clearly so that anyone can read and clearly understand the exact services or merchandise purchased.

STEP 7

The Careful Approach

- If you decide to prepay for your services, be sure you understand all arrangements and have them in writing.

- Ask any of the following questions that you feel are necessary:

  > Is my money 100 percent refundable at any time?

  > Can I transfer my arrangements without penalty?

> Where will my money be placed (bank, savings & loan, insurance, or trust)?

> Will I receive a receipt and proof of deposit after payment?

> What is your commission?

> What written guarantees do I have that my funds are available when needed?

> Is my account insured? If yes, by whom?

> Will I pay taxes on my earned interest?

> If your funeral home is sold, can I obtain or transfer my money without penalty?

> Is my money sheltered if I have to go on Medicaid?

> If you go out of business, what happens to my money?

> Are you licensed by the state? If yes, please provide proof, including your insurance identification number.

> If I cancel my arrangements several years from now, who keeps the earned interest?

- If the above questions are not answered to your satisfaction, **do not pay.** If the answers given are not in writing, **do not pay.** If you are pressured, **do not pay.** If you have not compared at least three firms, **do not pay.**

Cremation—With Memorial Service

STEP 1   Read the pros and cons of Cremation with Memorial Service

STEP 2   Determine if these arrangements meet the approval of survivors

STEP 3   Choose options

STEP 4   Detailed description of options

STEP 5   Gather price information

STEP 6   Compare prices, services, and attitudes of providers

STEP 7   Finalize arrangements

STEP 8   The careful approach

STEP 1

Pros

- Low cost. Purchase of an urn is optional.

- Saves land.

- Reduces or eliminates costs associated with burial: caskets, vaults, embalming, and cemetery services of opening and closing a grave.

- Provides the same elements valued in funeral services, without having the body present:

  > Allows flexible time scheduling (days, weeks, months) after one dies.

  > Simple to plan.

  > Does not require professional assistance (although it may be helpful in some cases).

  > Provides closure—a sense of finality.

  > Can be as simple or elaborate as one chooses.

  > Can include the use of many options such as music, flowers, photographs, and alternative site selection.

Cons

NOTE—In most states, the next of kin will be required to sign a "Cremation Authorization Form" provided by the funeral home, crematory, or both.

WARNING—Sometimes funeral directors or cremation society operators insist that a family identify the body before cremation and will attempt to sell the family an expensive container in which to view the deceased. If this occurs, request that the identification be made on their dressing table.

- Limits viewing the deceased. Anyone wanting to view the deceased would have to do so either at the place of death (i.e., hospital, nursing home) or at the funeral home's preparation facility, before the deceased is taken to the crematory.

- There may be a charge for private family viewing without embalming if they dress the body and set the features of the deceased.

- Some funeral homes limit the time permitted. Ask for an hourly rate, if so desired.

STEP 2

Approval of Survivors

- In a pre-need situation, determine if the arrangements you are making meet the approval of your next of kin or survivors. In some states, pre-arrangements can be changed by survivors after death has occurred. However, arrangements need not be altered if they are discussed and survivors understand your wishes while you are living.

- Planning a memorial service requires making phone calls and co-ordinating the efforts of a few people.

- You should consider your survivors' abilities to organize and conduct the memorial service without the aid of a funeral director. In Step 4 and on page 71, there is a list with explanations of each option they will face while planning a memorial service. People plan their own weddings; why not their funerals and memorials?

- While gathering price information, consider the cost of hiring a funeral director. Read Step 4: Detailed Description of Options, while planning a memorial service.

STEP 3

Choosing Options

- While reviewing the following options and making decisions regarding memorial services, determine if **YOU** want to organize the memorial service or hire a funeral director. Even if you hire a funeral director, many of the responsibilities and decisions will still be yours.

- When calling funeral homes for price information, ask for prices *with* and *without* their services for arranging and conducting memorial services. If you decide to plan and organize your own memorial service, see the following pages for help with the details:

    > Various services offered by the funeral home

    > Disposition of Ashes

    > Date and time of memorial service

    > Location of memorial service

> Use of clergy or speaker

> Number of people attending

> Music

> Private or public service

> Memorial accessories:
          —memorial folders
          —prayer cards
          —register book
          —thank-you notes

> Memorial announcement

> Obituary

> Greeters and ushers

> Flowers and choice of florist

> Luncheon following memorial service

> Pictures and memorabilia

> Visitation times before memorial service

> Military services

> Fraternal orders

STEP 4

Detailed Description of Options

Funeral Home Services

- The death of a family member, friend, or loved one will find you in no mood to make multitudes of difficult decisions. If you are responsible for making someone's funeral or memorial services, then pre-thinking and pre-planning your options—not pre-paying—is helpful.

- In Step 5, you will shop for the "best price" and the "best services." It will be difficult to put a dollar value on the compassion and care given to your family, so it is important to take a minute to think about your own situation and the assistance they will need before, during, and after the service.

- In addition to the basic services that all funeral homes offer, there are "additional" services made available by **some** funeral homes. In many cases, these services are the most appreciated functions a funeral home offers because they can make your family's burden more bearable.

- Assistance with Death Certificates: It will be necessary to notify various business and governmental agencies that death has occurred. The following list will help you decide how much assistance you may need to complete these tasks. Many funeral homes offer services for this and can be of invaluable assistance.

  > Real estate transfers

  > Probate court

  > Motor vehicles (cars, trucks, boats, etc.)

  > Banks, brokers, investments

  > Veterans affairs

  > Social security

  > Life insurance

  > Pension benefits

- **Some** funeral homes schedule a meeting with the family, providing clerical assistance and transportation to the above offices and agencies. If you need this service, inquire about the price and decide if the cost is worth the trouble it will save you and your survivors.

- Flower Delivery: Sometimes it is difficult to load all plants, flowers, etc., into your vehicles. Some funeral homes provide this in their professional services fees, while others will charge a separate fee.

- Meals: After the memorial service, the funeral director should be able to reserve or recommend a place that accommodates memorial luncheons.

- Hotel Accommodations: The funeral director should be able to recommend a nearby place that is within your budget and suitable to your needs.

- Survivors Workshops: The funeral director should be able to direct you to a group which assists survivors of suicide, sudden infant death, AIDS, etc. Hospitals, church groups, and non-profit organizations often sponsor these activities.

Disposition of Ashes

- Your options for disposition of ashes include, but are not limited to:

    > Scattering

    > Placing ashes in a Columbarium or Mausoleum niche

    > Burial in a cemetery. If you own cemetery property, check to see about its regulations and fees.

Urns

- There are very few requirements made to account for a family's disposition of ashes. Some states have laws that forbid scattering on public lands. Before purchasing an urn, consider what you will be doing with the ashes. It is not necessary or required by law to purchase an urn for any method of disposition. Urns are mostly used for display, at home or in a niche at a Columbarium. If a crematory or funeral home insists that you purchase an urn, you may provide your own container or vase, probably for much less money than the cost of those offered.

- Most crematories place the ashes in a plastic bag and then into a hard plastic box before giving them to the family or funeral director. *This container is suitable for burial and for holding the ashes until scattering is complete.*

Date and Time

- Before you set a date and time, make sure all facilities, people involved (family from out of town), clergy, luncheon facility, flower shop, etc. can accommodate or attend on that date and at that time. A few quick phone calls can prevent having to change plans at the last minute.

Location of Memorial Services

- Churches and funeral homes are common locations for memorial services. However, memorial services can be held anywhere people can gather, considering seating capacity, parking, time of year, and availability.

- Alternative locations for memorials:
    > Fraternal halls (e.g. Eagles, Moose, Elks)

    > Masonic Temple, Knights of Columbus Hall

    > Parks

    > Residence

    > Ocean side/lakeside

    > Favorite saloon

    > Golf course

    > University

- *Even if you are not a member, many churches will allow you to use their facility for a reasonable fee*—usually for much less than the cost of using a funeral home's facilities. Many churches have sound systems, plenty of seating, parking, and a place for a luncheon following the services.

Clergy or Speaker

- Consider what you want to be said and the desired formality of services **before** choosing your speaker or clergy. **Before** planning too far, check that the person is available. It is very important to give them a few written ideas of what you want to be said and the music to be played. It is highly recommended that you meet this person and make sure that they have a clear understanding of your expectations. If you want an upbeat, uplifting memorial with special music, say so.

Number of People

- Factors that determine the number of people attending a memorial service could be the age of the deceased, social and church involvement, achievements, and whether or not an obituary was placed in the paper. The reasons for needing to know approximately how many people will attend:
    > Number of memorial folders (optional)

    > Size and location of facility to be used

> Number of people for luncheon (optional)

> Assistance needed at memorial service

Music

- Music is often the most overlooked and under-utilized aspect of a memorial service. It can be very comforting and uplifting to use music in conjunction with the spoken message. By using "personal favorite" selections, whether they are traditional hymns, modern music, contemporary, jazz, country, rock, or spiritual, you will be adding beauty and meaning to the service. With some planning, such accompaniments as piano, violin, bagpipes, guitar, flute, or a soloist singing a favorite song can add a great deal to services that have traditionally been limited to traditional hymns.

- Some creative and memorable musical selections requested by families for memorial services have been: "Take Me Out To The Ball Game"; "My Way," by Frank Sinatra; "Somewhere Over The Rainbow," by Judy Garland; "Danny Boy," by Kate Smith; "Stairway To Heaven," by Led Zeppelin (used for a teenager killed in an auto accident); "Amazing Grace" (played on bagpipes); "Unforgettable," by Nat King Cole; "Evergreen," by Barbara Streisand; "Ave Maria," by Pavarotti; "Bridge Over Troubled Water," by Simon and Garfunkel; "Desperado," by The Eagles and "The National Anthem," by Arthur Fiedler and the Boston Philharmonic (Veterans Service).

- Most churches and funeral homes have the necessary sound equipment to play cassettes or compact discs, and given enough time, can arrange for musicians. If you are having services at an "alternative" site and would like a musician, call a church, college/university or an institute of music for a referral.

Private or Public Memorial Services

- Sometimes immediate friends and families can be more comforting than hoards of people you may not know, or may not care to see at that time. If you opt for a private memorial service, mention it in the obituary or do not run an obituary until after the service is held.

Memorial Accessories

- Memorial Folders: Memorial folders are traditionally used for Protestant services, and are available through funeral homes, some church supply stores, and printers. Their purpose is debatable, since most end up left on church pews or folded up in a pocket, later to be discarded.

- Prayer Cards: Prayer cards are traditionally used for Catholic and Orthodox faiths and are available through funeral homes, some church supply stores, and printers.

- Register Books: Register books are especially helpful if they have name and address lines to aid in sending "thank-you" notes, if so desired. Register books are frequently sold at funeral homes for $25.00 to $65.00, and similar products are available for much less through stationary and church supply stores.

- Thank-you Notes: Thank-you notes are usually sent to those that pay a special kindness to you such as sending flowers, making memorial contributions to charitable organizations, assisting in memorial services, and providing food for a luncheon. They are available at funeral homes, stationary stores, and card shops. It is usually worth shopping around; sometimes selections offered at funeral homes are limited and expensive.

Memorial Announcement

- Using a memorial announcement can be an appropriate, effective, and inexpensive method of notifying a selective group of people that someone has died. Memorial announcements can be personalized to meet each family's needs. It can be very effective for notifying friends and family who live far away. **Take this book with you to a PRINTER and show them exactly what you want from the Memorial Announcement samples on page 149.**

Obituaries

- These can include a wide variety of information useful in notifying friends, family, and business associates. They are especially helpful when they include specific information about visitation times, location, date, time of services, and a listing of charitable organizations where contributions may be sent (see page 147).

Greeters/Ushers

- Greeters and ushers can be members of the family or close friends who are willing to help greet people, hang coats, ask visitors to sign the register book, and hand out memorial folders or prayer cards.

Florist

- Similar to music, flowers are one of the most overlooked options of a memorial service. Many florists simply do not have experience or talent advising families about the use of flowers in conjunction with memorial services. When meeting with the florist, consider the following: Pictures, memorabilia, size of facility, and flower stands available through the florist or the funeral home. By using a competent florist who is interested in working with the aforementioned elements, flowers can add beauty and warmth to the memorial service.

Luncheon

- Serving lunch after a memorial service is sometimes quite nice, whether you serve coffee and pastry or a multi-course meal provided by a top-notch restaurant or caterer. Luncheons offer a chance for friends to talk and families to come together, which may begin the process of healing.

Use of Pictures, Videos, or Memorabilia

- Pictures taken throughout a person's life can be very important and meaningful in terms of comforting a family. You can use pictures, photographs, and videos to remember a person when they were happy, successful, content, in love, proud; the list is endless. Such pictures can be more meaningful than viewing a body which, due to injury or illness, is not what you care to remember.

Visitation

- Consider allowing a period of time before or after the service to visit with friends and family. If you are having an obituary printed, it is suggested that such times be listed.

Military Services

- If a person served during a time of war and was honorably discharged from the military, he or she should be entitled to military services. The local Veterans of Foreign Wars organization (V.F.W.) can usually arrange for a graveside service including a chaplain, bugler, honor guard, and gun salute.

Fraternal/Religious Organization Services

- There are too many to list, but if a person had a strong affiliation with such organizations as the Masons, Demolay, or Knights of Columbus, they will quite often have a memorial service at the funeral home the evening before the funeral service if you so choose.

STEP 5

Gather Price Information

NOTE—If you don't ask, you could be comparing prices from the same firm, which could lead you to believe that prices must be consistent across the board.

- Using the Telephone Checklist on the next page and the Yellow Page section of your phone book, call at least three funeral homes for price information. When calling, ask each funeral home if they are associated with or co-owned by any other funeral homes in your area. It is common for a conglomerate to own several funeral homes and cemeteries in an area and operate under different names.

- It is required by law in all 50 states that price information be given over the phone.

- Surveys have shown that prices can range considerably in areas with little competition. Don't be hesitant to call for prices in neighboring communities. The savings may be well worth the call.

- If you prefer, visit the funeral homes of choice and request a **General Price List**. *It is required by law that upon request, General Price Lists be given to the public.*

Telephone Checklist

NOTE: It is very important to obtain accurate prices for the services you desire, so request totals. Bait and switch discrepancies may arise during final arrangements if you don't obtain exact price quotes in the beginning.

I am calling for price information for cremation with a memorial service to be held at

_____

(name of funeral home or church)

	Company Example	Company A	Company B	Company C
Funeral Home Name:	Sunset			
Funeral Home Representative:	John Doe			
Date:	9/01/02			
Phone Number:	810-230-0000			
	PRICES	PRICES	PRICES	PRICES
Basic Services of Funeral Director & Staff:	$500*			
Conducting Memorial Service—Optional:	$300*			
Private Family Viewing	$0*			
Use of Funeral Home for Memorial—Optional:	$150*			
Removal from Place of Death:	$100*			
Transportation to Crematory:	$100*			
Other:				
TOTAL OF SERVICES:	$1,150*			
Cremation Container:	$50*			
Urn—Optional:	$100*			
Register Book:	$25*			
Memorial Folders/Prayer Cards:	$25*			
Thank-you Notes:	$15*			
Other:				
TOTAL OF MERCHANDISE:	$215*			
TOTAL OF SERVICES & MERCHANDISE:	$1365*			
Total Without Use of Funeral Home for Memorial:	$1,215*			
Total Without Use of Funeral Director and Funeral Home for Memorial:	$915*			

* The prices above are meant to be merely examples

Additional Expenses—Not Necessary to Compare—Obtain Prices only for Planning Final Cost

Additional Expenses	Example	Price
Cremation—Crematory	$150*	
Option of Obituary	$100*	
Number of Death Certificates (5)	$30*	
Musicians/organist/soloist	$100*	
Clergy	$100*	
Church Fees:	No Charge*	
Luncheon:	$250*	
Memorial Announcement:	$25*	
Florist:	$200*	
Other:	None*	
TOTAL ADDITIONAL EXPENSES:	$955*	
TOTAL FROM PREVIOUS PAGE:	$1,365*	
TOTAL SERVICES, MERCHANDISE, AND ADDITIONAL EXPENSES:	$2,320*	

* The prices above are meant to be merely examples

These expenses will primarily be the same for all funeral homes, but knowing their prices will help determine total costs. If these expenses are added into your contract, you may be paying an extra fee, or the funeral home may receive a discount for completing these services.

STEP 6

Compare Prices

- Compare funeral homes' prices and their willingness to serve you.

- How willing is a funeral home to tailor services that meet your needs? If they are not willing, choose another. Funeral directors will bend over backwards if they can take a consumer away from a competitor.

- You do not have to purchase all merchandise and services from one funeral home. Ask for a package discount if you do purchase all services and merchandise from the same location.

- Inspect facilities for cleanliness, adequate parking, and handicap accessibility. Ask to see the area where your service will be held and ask about their ability to assist you with music selections or other options you have chosen.

STEP 7

Finalize Arrangements and Services

NOTE—Final arrangements should be written so that anyone can read and clearly understand the exact services or merchandise purchased. Compare their General Price List with the prices given over the phone. Do this prior to any conversation regarding services or merchandise. If there are any differences or if you are not satisfied, request an explanation. If you are still not satisfied, leave. It may be necessary to report them to the Federal Trade Commission. Funeral Homes are responsible for all employees who quote prices, and can be held accountable.

- Make an appointment to meet with the funeral home of your choice. Take this guide along with the following:

  > Completed obituary form (page 147)—optional

  > Completed death certificate form (page 151)

  > List of options you will use (see Step 3).

  > If you need assistance locating clergy, a soloist, or if you have questions regarding death certificates, now is the time to inquire.

STEP 8

The Careful Approach

- *If you decide to prepay your services, be sure you understand all arrangements and have them in writing.*

- Ask any of the following questions that you feel are necessary:

  > Is my money 100 percent refundable at any time?

  > Can I transfer my arrangements without penalty?

  > Where will my money be placed (bank, savings & loan, insurance, or trust)?

  > Will I receive a receipt and proof of deposit after payment?

  > What is your commission?

  > What written guarantees do I have that my funds are available when needed?

  > Is my account insured? If yes, by whom?

  > Will I pay taxes on my earned interest?

  > If your funeral home is sold, can I obtain or transfer my money without penalty?

  > Is my money sheltered if I have to go on Medicaid?

  > If you go out of business, what happens to my money?

  > Are you licensed by the state? If yes, please provide proof, including your insurance identification number.

  > If I cancel my arrangements several years from now, who keeps the earned interest?

- If the above questions are not answered to your satisfaction, **do not pay.** If the answers given are not in writing, **do not pay.** If you are pressured, **do not pay.** If you have not compared at least three firms, **do not pay.**

EXAMPLE—Memorial Service Planner

This planner is to be utilized for planning memorial services, in lieu of hiring a funeral director.

	ARRANGEMENT DETAILS	ARRANGED OR CONFIRMED BY	PAYMENT
Time/Date	1:00 p.m. Wednesday, August 26	Confirmed by Church Secretary	Not Applicable
Place	First United Methodist Church	Rev. Jones	No Charge/member*
Church Phone #	(612) 659-1000	Parish Office	Not Applicable
Clergy/Speaker	Reverend Jones	Rev. Jones	$100.00—PAID*
Meeting w/family	5:00 p.m., Tuesday, August 25	Rev. Jones	Not Applicable
Music	Piano music before/after services	Church music dir.	$50.00—PAID*
Soloist	Mr. Graham from church	Mr. Graham	$50.00—PAID*
Special Songs/Tape	"Amazing Grace", "Danny Boy"	Music Dir. has music	Not Applicable
Register Book	Sunset Funeral Home	Purchased at Funeral Home	$25.00—PAID*
Memorial Programs	Handled by Sunset Funeral Home	Sunset Funeral Home	$25.00—PAID*
Thank you notes	Purchased at funeral home	Sunset Funeral Home	$15.00—PAID*
Obituary	One day, local paper	Placed in paper by Sunset Funeral Home	$100.00—PAID*
Visitation Times	Noon–1:00 p.m., August 26	Times confirmed by church secretary	Not Applicable
Veteran Services	Not a Veteran	Not a Veteran	Not Applicable
Flag	None	Not chosen	Not Applicable
Masonic or Knights of Columbus	Not a member	Not a member	Not Applicable
Florist	Elegant Florist	Ordered from Larry, August 24	$200.00—PAID*
Luncheon	Following memorial at church social hall	Church secretary confirmed	Included in payment to church*
Caterer	Complete catering (50–75 people)	Mr. Young confirmed	$250.00—PAID*
Church Setup	Pictures and memorabilia on communion table		
Greeters/Ushers	Uncle Ed and Uncle Harold	Aunt Charlene	No Charge*
Memorial Announcement	Ordered through Kinko's Printers	Mr. O'Leary at Kinko's Printers	$25.00—PAID*
Disposition of Ashes	Scattering at cabin	Next Week	Not applicable
Miscellaneous	Make room reservations for out-of-town family members (20 people)	Made reservations for 20 people	Paid by individual family members*

* The prices above are meant to be merely examples

Memorial Service Planner

This planner is to be utilized for planning memorial services, in lieu of hiring a funeral director.

	ARRANGEMENT DETAILS	ARRANGED/CONFIRMEDBY	PAYMENT
TIME/DATE			
PLACE			
CHURCH PHONE #			
CLERGY/SPEAKER			
MEETING W/FAMILY			
MUSIC			
SOLOIST			
SPECIAL SONGS/TAPE			
REGISTER BOOK			
MEMORIAL PROGRAMS			
URN			
THANK-YOU NOTES			
OBITUARY			
VISITATION TIMES			
VETERAN SERVICES			
FLAG			
MASONIC / KNIGHTS OF COLUMBUS			
FLORIST			
LUNCHEON			
CATERER			
CHURCH SETUP			
GREETERS/ USHERS			
MEMORIAL ANNOUNCEMENT			
DISPOSITION OF ASHES			
MISCELLANEOUS			

Cremation—With Funeral Service

STEP 1 Read the pros and cons of Cremation with Funeral Services

STEP 2 Determine if these services meet the approval of survivors

STEP 3 Choose options

STEP 4 Detailed description of options

STEP 5 Gather price information

STEP 6 Compare prices, services, and attitudes of funeral providers

STEP 7 Finalize arrangements

STEP 8 The careful approach

STEP 1

Pros

- Saves land.

- Lower cost alternative to burial. Eliminates the cost of a vault, opening and closing a grave, and the purchase of a grave, if you scatter the ashes.

- Allows for viewing the deceased.

- Cremation caskets provide an inexpensive option to traditional caskets.

Cons

NOTE—In most states, the next of kin will be required to sign a "Cremation Authorization Form" provided by the funeral home, crematory, or both.

- Not all funeral homes offer rental caskets or cremation caskets, although they are available to all funeral homes.

- Some people are opposed to cremation.

- The expense of a casket, urn, embalming/preparation, and use of a funeral home.

STEP 2

Approval of Survivor(s)

- In a pre-need situation, determine if the arrangements you are making meet the approval of your next of kin or survivors. In some states, survivors can change pre-arrangements after death has occurred. However, arrangements need not be altered if they are discussed and survivors understand your wishes while you are living.

STEP 3

Choosing Options

- Preplanning is the most important part of making pre-arrangements, not prepaying.

    > Various services offered by funeral homes

    > Casket selection

> Disposition of ashes

> Cemetery selection

> Monument or marker

> Flowers

> Memorial announcement

> Obituary

> Having an open or closed casket

> Use of clergy or speaker

> Date and time

> Location of funeral

> Number of people attending

> Music

> Private or public services

> Funeral accessories

> Luncheon following funeral service

> Pictures and memorabilia

> Visitation times before funeral

> Military services

> Fraternal organization services

> Greeters or ushers

STEP 4

Detailed Description of Options

Funeral Home Services

- The death of a family member, friend, or loved one will find you in no mood to make multitudes of difficult decisions. If you are responsible for making someone's funeral or memorial services, then pre-planning your options—not pre-paying—is helpful.

- In Step 5, you will shop for the "best price" and the "best services." It will be difficult to put a dollar value on the compassion and care given to your family, so it is important to take a minute to think about your own situation and the assistance they will need before, during, and after the service.

- In addition to the basic services that all funeral homes offer, there are "additional" services made available by **some** funeral homes. In many cases, these services are the most appreciated functions a funeral home offers because they can make your family's burden more bearable.

- Assistance with Death Certificates: It will be necessary to notify various business and governmental agencies that death has occurred. The following list will help you decide how much assistance you may need to complete these tasks. Many funeral homes offer services for this and can be of invaluable assistance.

  > Real estate transfers

  > Probate court

  > Motor vehicles (cars, trucks, boats, etc.)

  > Banks, brokers, investments

  > Veterans' affairs

  > Social security

  > Life insurance

  > Pension benefits

- **Some** funeral homes schedule a meeting with the family, providing clerical assistance and transportation to offices or agencies. If you need this service, inquire about the price and decide if the cost is worth the trouble it will save you and your survivors.

- Flower Delivery: Sometimes it is difficult to load all plants, flowers, etc., into your vehicles. Some funeral homes provide this in their professional services fees, while others will charge a separate fee.

- Meals: After the burial, the funeral director should be able to reserve or recommend a place that accommodates funeral or memorial luncheons.

- Hotel Accommodations: The funeral director should be able to recommend a nearby place that is within your budget and suitable to your needs.

- Survivors Workshops: The funeral director should be able to direct you to a group which assists survivors of suicide, sudden infant death, AIDS, etc. Hospitals, church groups, and non-profit organizations often sponsor these activities.

Casket Selection

- Depending upon where you live, there are various options as to where you can buy a casket. Check the Yellow Page section of your telephone directory for any of the following:

  > funeral homes

  > cemeteries

  > retail casket stores

- *Caskets*—Before you attempt to select and compare casket prices, you will need some basic product information. Casket materials greatly affect their cost.

- Rental Caskets or Ceremonial Caskets—Wooden or metal exteriors with a removable lightweight wood interior and upholstery like traditional caskets. Unfortunately for the consumer, not many funeral homes carry much of a selection, and the casket manufacturers have not done much to promote these economical, practical alternative caskets.

  > Wooden caskets—Price is usually determined by what kind of wood is used and how ornately the interior and exterior are finished.
  >> —Walnut or Mahogany—Most expensive
  >> —Cherry
  >> —Birch, Maple, Oak
  >> —Pine
  >> —Poplar
  >> —Veneer—Least expensive

  > The 20-gauge steel caskets often look cheap, but with flowers, a flag, or pictures on the lid, they do the job.

WARNINGS
- Compare prices carefully. Prices vary based on workmanship and materials.
- When pre-purchasing ask for a guarantee *in writing* that you will get your money or merchandise back if that business fails.
- Casket designs and models do change with time. Ask for a guarantee *in writing* that you will receive the manufacturer and the quality you have chosen.
- Some funeral homes offer "packages" that allow for "discounts" when all merchandise and services are purchased from them. Ask about these package deals
- Prices can vary hundreds of dollars between dealers for the same merchandise.

> Steel caskets: Made in three thicknesses:

—16-gauge steel—the most lavish and expensive steel casket

—18-gauge steel—moderately expensive

—20-gauge steel—thinnest, least expensive steel

> Copper caskets: Generally half the price of bronze, but still quite expensive.

> Bronze caskets: The most expensive metal casket, usually quite lavish, with high grade velvet interior.

Disposition of Ashes

- Your options for disposition of ashes include, but are not limited to:

   > Scattering

   > Placing ashes in a Columbarium or Mausoleum niche

   > Burial in a cemetery. If you own cemetery property, check to see about its regulations and fees.

   > Veterans have cemetery benefits: 1-800-827-1000

- There are very few requirements made to account for a family's disposition of ashes. Some states have laws that forbid scattering. Before purchasing an urn, consider what you will be doing with the ashes. It is not necessary or required by law to purchase an urn for any method of disposition. Urns are mostly used for display, at home or in a niche at a Columbarium. If a crematory or funeral home insists that you purchase an urn, you may provide your own container or vase, probably for much less money than the cost of those offered.

- Most crematories place the ashes in a plastic bag and then into a hard plastic box before giving them to the family or funeral director. *This container is suitable for burial and for holding the ashes until scattering is complete.*

Cemetery Selection

- The most important consideration when purchasing a gravesite or a niche in a Columbarium is the financial condition of the cemetery and its continuing ability to maintain the grounds or facilities to meet your standards.

- Do not hesitate to ask about their perpetual care funds. These funds are set aside for the future maintenance of the grounds and facilities.

- Consider all costs before purchasing anything. Remember, it is very difficult to get what you originally paid for cemetery property when reselling.

  > Cost of niche or grave

  > Opening and closing the niche or grave

Monument or marker

- A monument is above ground level, while a marker is flat. Prices vary considerably and are worth comparing.

Flowers

- Similar to music, flowers are one of the most overlooked options of a memorial service. Many florists simply do not have experience or talent advising families about the use of flowers in conjunction with memorial services. When meeting with the florist, consider the following: Pictures, memorabilia, size of facility, and flower stands available through the florist or the funeral home. By using a competent florist who is interested in working with the aforementioned elements, flowers can add beauty and warmth to the memorial service.

Memorial Announcement

- A memorial announcement can be an appropriate, effective, and inexpensive method to notify a selective group of people that someone has died. Memorial announcements may be personalized to meet each family's needs. It can be very effective for notifying friends and family who live far away. *Take this book with you to a PRINTER and show them exactly what you want, using the enclosed samples of memorial announcements in this guide (see page 149).*

Obituary

- Obituaries can include a wide variety of information useful in notifying friends, family, and business associates. They are especially helpful when they include specific information about visitation times, location, date, time of services, and a listing of charitable organizations where contributions may be sent (see page 147).

Open or closed casket

- If the deceased has deteriorated in appearance, a framed picture sitting on a closed casket may be the best choice.

Clergy or speaker

- Consider what you want to be said and the desired formality of services **before** choosing your speaker or clergy. **Before** planning too far, check that the person is available. It is very important to give them a few written ideas of what you want to be said and the music to be played. It is highly recommended that you meet this person and make sure that they have a clear understanding of your expectations. If you want an upbeat, uplifting memorial with special music, say so.

Date and time

- Before you set a date and time, make sure all facilities, people involved (family from out of town), clergy, luncheon facility, flower shop, etc., can accommodate or attend on that date and at that time. A few quick calls can prevent changing plans at the last minute.

Location of Funeral

- Churches and funeral homes are common locations for funeral services. However, funerals can be held anywhere people can gather, considering seating capacity, parking, time of year, and availability.

- *Even if you are not a member, many churches will allow you to use their facility for a reasonable fee*—usually for much less than the cost of using a funeral home's facilities. Many churches have sound systems, plenty of seating, parking, and a place for a luncheon following the services.

Number of People

- Factors that determine the number of people attending a funeral service could be the age of the deceased, social and church involvement, achievements, and whether or not an obituary was placed in the paper. The reasons for needing to know approximately how many people will attend:

  > Number of memorial folders (optional)

  > Size and location of facility to be used

  > Number of people for luncheon (optional)

  > Assistance needed at funeral service

Music

- Music is often the most overlooked and under-utilized aspect of a funeral service. It can be very comforting and uplifting to use music in conjunction with the spoken message. By using "personal favorite" selections, whether they are traditional hymns, modern music, contemporary, jazz, country, rock, or spiritual, you will be adding beauty and meaning to the service. With some planning, such accompaniments as piano, violin, bagpipes, guitar, flute, or a soloist singing a favorite song can add a great deal to services that have traditionally been limited to traditional hymns.

- Some creative and memorable musical selections requested by families for funerals have been: "Take Me Out To The Ball Game"; "My Way," by Frank Sinatra; "Somewhere Over The Rainbow," by Judy Garland; "Danny Boy," by Kate Smith; "Stairway To Heaven," by Led Zeppelin (used for a teenager killed in an auto accident); "Amazing Grace" (played on bagpipes); "Unforgettable," by Nat King Cole; "Evergreen," by Barbara Streisand; "Ave Maria," by Pavarotti; "Bridge Over Troubled Water," by Simon and Garfunkel; "Desperado," by The Eagles and "The National Anthem," by Arthur Fiedler and the Boston Philharmonic (Veterans Service).

- Most churches and funeral homes have the necessary sound equipment to play cassettes or compact discs, and given enough time, can arrange for musicians. If you are having services at an "alternative" site and would like a musician, call a church, college/university or an institute of music for a referral.

Private or Public Services

- Sometimes immediate friends and families can be more comforting than hoards of people you may not know, or may not care to see at that time. If you opt for a private funeral service, mention it in the obituary or do not run an obituary until after the service is held.

Funeral Accessories

- Memorial Folders: Memorial folders are traditionally used for Protestant services, and are available through funeral homes, some church supply stores, and printers. Their purpose is debatable, since most end up left on church pews or folded up in a pocket, later to be discarded.

- Prayer Cards: Prayer cards are traditionally used for Catholic and Orthodox faiths and are available through funeral homes, some church supply stores, and printers.

- Register Books: Register books are especially helpful if they have name and address lines to aid in sending "thank-you" notes, if so desired. Register books are frequently sold at funeral homes for $25.00 to $65.00, and similar products are available for much less through stationary and church supply stores.

- Thank-you Notes: Thank-you notes are usually sent to those that pay a special kindness to you such as sending flowers, making memorial contributions to charitable organizations, assisting in funeral services, and providing food for a luncheon. They are available at funeral homes, stationary stores, and card shops. It is usually worth shopping around; sometimes selections offered at funeral homes are limited and expensive.

Luncheon

- Serving lunch after a funeral is sometimes quite nice, whether you serve coffee and pastry or a multi-course meal provided by a top-notch restaurant or caterer. They offer a chance for friends to talk and families to come together, which may begin the process of healing.

Use of Pictures, Videos, or Memorabilia

- Pictures taken throughout a person's life can be very important and meaningful in terms of comforting a family. You can use pictures, photographs, and videos to remember a person when they were happy, successful, content, in love, proud; the list is endless. Such pictures can be more meaningful than viewing a body which, due to injury or illness, is not what you care to remember.

Visitation

- Consider allowing a period of time before or after the service to visit with friends and family. If you are having an obituary printed, it is suggested that such times be listed.

Military Services

- If a person served during a time of war and was honorably discharged from the military, he or she should be entitled to military services. The local Veterans of Foreign Wars organization (V.F.W.) can usually arrange for a graveside service including a chaplain, bugler, honor guard, and gun salute.

Fraternal/Religious Organization Services

- There are too many to list, but if a person had a strong affiliation with such organizations as the Masons, Demolay, or Knights of Columbus, they will quite often have a memorial service at the funeral home the evening before the funeral service if you so choose.

Greeters/Ushers

- Greeters and ushers can be members of the family or close friends who are willing to help greet people, hang coats, ask visitors to sign the register book, and hand out memorial folders or prayer cards.

STEP 5

**Gather Price
Information**

- Start by selecting one funeral home as a "guinea pig" for collecting pricing and product information. Later, you will make telephone calls to other funeral homes, casket stores and other related businesses to gather prices for comparison. Select your guinea pig carefully using recommendations from reliable sources such as family, clergy, or business associates. Look for a privately owned funeral home if possible.

  > While at the funeral home, discuss the services you are interested in and any options associated with them. Talk specifically about their services, including assistance after the funeral or memorial if desired and the cost of what you are planning.

  > After you clearly understand what services you are selecting, ask for the price with subtractions made for services you do not desire. Make sure you obtain prices for everything you will need.

  > Remember, the funeral home must give you a price list for their services for you to take home. Make sure you understand it thoroughly and keep it for further price comparison.

  > After you have completed your shopping trip to the guinea pig funeral home and have their prices for their services and other products, your next step is to use the telephone to go comparison-shopping.

  > Try to narrow down your choices of caskets to make comparison-shopping easier.

Casket Shopping Strategy At the Guinea Pig

- Your objective is to find a casket you like, find out what it costs, and how cooperative a particular business is in finding a casket that suits your needs.

- Look at their casket price list and notice which price range has the largest selection of caskets. Usually they will list a few very cheap ones and a few very expensive ones, with the majority somewhere in between.

- Funeral homes and casket stores do this to create an average price image in the customer's mind. They also offer the most selection in the price range from which they want you to buy.

- If, for example, you want an inexpensive wooden casket, and there isn't one on the price list, ask to see one. If you are not satisfied with their response, ask to see the manufacturer catalog. Batesville, the largest casket manufacturer, carries close to 100 steel caskets and over 30 wooden caskets.

- If you request a bronze casket, they'll deliver it on Easter Sunday. You should expect the same service if you choose a less expensive wooden or metal casket.

- If your first funeral home selection does not prove to be worthwhile, due to lack of cooperation or willingness to help you, move on.

- Once you have chosen a casket, ask for and write down very carefully the manufacturer, the model number, the model name, and the price. You will need this information later while comparison-shopping by phone.

- Casket names are intentionally changed by funeral homes to avoid comparison-shopping, so be able to describe in detail the casket in which you are interested.

- Using the Telephone Checklist on the next page and the Yellow Page section of your phone book, call at least three funeral homes for price information. When calling, ask each funeral home if they are associated with or co-owned by any other funeral homes in your area. It is common for a conglomerate to own several funeral homes and cemeteries in an area and operate under different names.

- It is required by law in all 50 states that price information be given over the phone.

- Surveys have shown that prices can range considerably in areas with little competition. Don't be hesitant to call for prices in neighboring communities. The savings may be well worth the call.

- If you prefer, visit the funeral homes of choice and request a **General Price List**. *It is required by law that upon request, General Price Lists be given to the public.*

NOTE—If you don't ask, you could be comparing prices from the same firm, which could lead you to believe that prices must be consistent across the board.

Telephone Checklist

NOTE: It is very important to obtain accurate prices for the services you desire, so request totals. Bait and switch discrepancies may arise during final arrangements if you don't obtain exact price quotes in the beginning.

I would like price information for funeral services held at

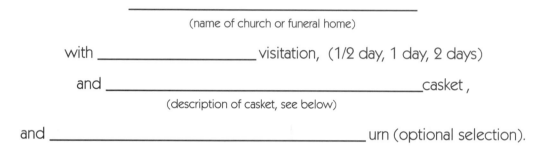

_____
(name of church or funeral home)

with _____ visitation, (1/2 day, 1 day, 2 days)

and _____casket ,
(description of casket, see below)

and _____ urn (optional selection).

Description of Casket—Urn—Selected at "Guinea Pig" Funeral Home

	Manufacturer	Name	Type	Model
Casket Example:	Batesville	Pacific Pine	pine	16 P1
1.				
2.				
3.				

USE FORM ON FOLLOWING PAGE

Telephone Checklist

	Company Example	Company A	Company B	Company C
Funeral Home Name:	Sunset			
Funeral Home Representative:	John Doe			
Date:	9/01/02			
Phone Number:	810-230-0000			
	PRICES	PRICES	PRICES	PRICES
Basic Services of Funeral Director & Staff:	$500*			
Conducting Funeral Ceremony— (church or chapel):	$300*			
Embalming (optional):	Not chosen*			
Other preparation:	Not chosen*			
Use of Facilities for Service:	$150*			
Use of Facilities for Viewing:	$150*			
Removal from Place of Death:	$100*			
Transportation to Crematory:	$100*			
Other Services	None chosen*			
TOTAL OF SERVICES:	$1,300*			
Casket:	$1,100*			
Casket Description (Name):	Batesville Pacific Pine			
Urn—Optional:	None selected*			
Register Book:	$25*			
Service Folders/Prayer Cards:	$25*			
Thank-you Notes:	$15*			
Other:				
TOTAL OF MERCHANDISE:	$1,165*			
TOTAL SERVICES AND MERCHANDISE:	$2,465*			

* The prices above are meant to be merely examples

Additional Expenses—Not Necessary to Compare—Obtain Prices only for Planning Final Cost

Additional Expenses	Example	Price
Crematory:	$150*	
Obituary:	$100*	
Number of Death Certificates (5):	$30*	
Clergy/Church:	$100*	
Musicians/organist/soloist:	$100*	
Memorial Announcements:	$25*	
Hair Preparation:	0*	
Luncheon:	$250*	
Permits:	0*	
Transportation of Deceased—Airline ets.	0*	
Florist:	$200*	
Other:		
TOTAL ADDITIONAL EXPENSES:	$955*	
TOTAL FROM PREVIOUS PAGE:	$2.465*	
TOTAL SERVICES, MERCHANDISE, AND ADDITIONAL EXPENSES:	$3,420*	

* The prices above are meant to be merely examples

These expenses will primarily be the same for all funeral homes, but knowing their prices will help determine total costs. If these expenses are added into your contract, you may be paying an extra fee, or the funeral home may receive a discount for completing these services.

STEP 6

Compare Prices

- Compare funeral homes' prices and their willingness to serve you.

- How willing is a funeral home to order a casket or urn, and tailor services that meet your needs? If they are not willing, choose another. Funeral directors will bend over backwards if they can take a consumer away from a competitor.

- You do not have to purchase all merchandise and services from one funeral home. Ask for a package discount if you do purchase all services, casket, and urn from the same location.

- Inspect facilities for cleanliness, adequate parking, and handicap accessibility. Ask to see the area where your service will be held and ask about their ability to assist you with music selections or other options you have chosen.

STEP 7

Finalize Arrangements

NOTE—Final arrangements should be written so that anyone can read and clearly understand the exact services or merchandise purchased. Compare their General Price List with the prices given over the phone. Do this prior to any conversation regarding services or merchandise. If there are any differences or if you are not satisfied, request an explanation. If you are still not satisfied, leave. It may be necessary to report them to the Federal Trade Commission. Funeral Homes are responsible for all employees who quote prices, and can be held accountable.

- Make an appointment to meet with the funeral home of your choice. Take this guide along with the following:

    › Completed obituary form (page 147)—optional

    › Completed death certificate form (page 151)

    › List of options you will use (see Step 3).

    › Casket or merchandise choices.

    › If you need assistance locating clergy, a soloist, or if you have questions regarding death certificates, now is the time to inquire.

STEP 8

The Careful Approach

- *If you decide to prepay your services, be sure you understand all arrangements and have them in writing.*

- Ask any of the following questions that you feel are necessary:

  > Is my money 100 percent refundable at any time?

  > Can I transfer my arrangements without penalty?

  > Where will my money be placed (bank, savings & loan, insurance, or trust) ?

  > Will I receive a receipt and proof of deposit after payment?

  > What is your commission?

  > What written guarantees do I have that my funds are available when needed?

  > Is my account insured? If yes, by whom?

  > Will I pay taxes on my earned interest?

  > If your funeral home is sold, can I obtain or transfer my money without penalty?

  > Is my money sheltered if I have to go on Medicaid?

  > If you go out of business, what happens to my money?

  > Are you licensed by the state? If yes, please provide proof, including your insurance identification number.

  > If I cancel my arrangements several years from now, who keeps the earned interest?

- If the above questions are not answered to your satisfaction, **do not pay**. If the answers given are not in writing, **do not pay**. If you are pressured, **do not pay**. If you have not compared at least three firms, **do not pay.**

Burial—No Service

STEP 1

Pros	• Low cost alternative to traditional funerals.
	• May be followed by memorial service at a later date, more convenient for the family.
	• Does not require embalming.
	• Basic, inexpensive caskets can be used without concern for public attitude or opinion.

Cons	• The added cost of a casket, vault, grave, and opening and closing grave, versus cremation.

STEP 2

Approval of Survivors	• In a pre-need situation, determine if the arrangements you are making meet the approval of your next of kin or survivors. In some states, survivors can change pre-arrangements after death has occurred. However, arrangements need not be altered if they are discussed and survivors understand your wishes while you are living.

STEP 3

Choose Options	• Various services offered by funeral home
	• Casket selection
	• Outer burial container (vault) selection
	• Cemetery selection
	• Monument or marker
	• Flowers
	• Memorial announcement
	• Obituary

STEP 4

Detailed Description of Options

Funeral Home Services

- The death of a family member, friend, or loved one will find you in no mood to make multitudes of difficult decisions. If you are responsible for making someone's funeral or memorial services, then pre-thinking your options—not pre-paying—is helpful.

- In Step 5, you will shop for the "best price" and the "best services." It will be difficult to put a dollar value on the compassion and care given to your family, so it is important to take a minute to think about your own situation and the assistance they will need before, during, and after the service.

- In addition to the basic services that all funeral homes offer, there are "additional" services made available by **some** funeral homes. In many cases, these services are the most appreciated functions a funeral home offers because they can make your family's burden more bearable.

- Assistance with Death Certificates: It will be necessary to notify various business and governmental agencies that death has occurred. The following list will help you decide how much assistance you may need to complete these tasks. Many funeral homes offer services for this and can be of invaluable assistance.

    > Real estate transfers

    > Probate court

    > Motor vehicles (cars, trucks, boats, etc.)

    > Banks, brokers, investments

    > Veterans' affairs: 1-800-827-1000

    > Social security

    > Life insurance

    > Pension benefits

- **Some** funeral homes schedule a meeting with the family, providing clerical assistance and transportation to offices or agencies. If you need this service, inquire about the price and decide if the cost is worth the trouble it will save you and your survivors.

- Flower Delivery: Sometimes it is difficult to load all plants, flowers, etc., into your vehicles. Some funeral homes provide this in their professional services fees, while others will charge a separate fee.

- Meals: After the burial, the funeral director should be able to reserve or recommend a place that accommodates funeral or memorial luncheons.

- Hotel Accommodations: The funeral director should be able to recommend a nearby place that is within your budget and suitable to your needs.

- Survivors Workshops: The funeral director should be able to direct you to a group which assists survivors of suicide, sudden infant death, AIDS, etc. Hospitals, church groups, and non-profit organizations often sponsor these activities.

Casket Selection

- Depending upon where you live, there are various options as to where you can buy a casket. Check the Yellow Page section of your telephone directory for any of the following:

  > funeral homes

  > cemeteries

  > retail casket stores

- *Caskets*—Before you attempt to select and compare casket prices, you will need some basic product information. Casket materials greatly affect their cost.

  > Bronze caskets: The most expensive metal casket, usually quite lavish, with high grade velvet interior.

  > Copper caskets: Generally half the price of bronze, but still quite expensive.

  > Steel caskets: Made in three thicknesses:
  >> —16-gauge steel—the most lavish and expensive steel casket
  >> —18-gauge steel—moderately expensive
  >> —20-gauge steel—thinnest, least expensive steel

WARNINGS—
- Compare prices carefully. Prices vary based on workmanship and materials.
- When pre-purchasing ask for a guarantee **in writing** that you will get your money or merchandise back if that business fails.
- Casket designs and models do change with time. Ask for a guarantee **in writing** that you will receive the manufacturer and the quality you have chosen.
- Some funeral homes offer "packages" that allow for "discounts" when all merchandise and services are purchased from them. Ask about these package deals.
- Prices can vary hundreds of dollars between dealers for the same merchandise.

> The 20-gauge steel caskets often look cheap, but with flowers, a flag, or pictures on the lid, they do the job.

> Remember that no casket will preserve or maintain the human body, regardless of what a funeral director or casket manufacturer claims. If such claims are made, ask for proof!

> Wooden caskets—Price is usually determined by what kind of wood is used and how ornately the interior and exterior are finished.
> —Walnut or Mahogany—Most expensive
> —Cherry
> —Birch, Maple, Oak
> —Pine
> —Poplar
> —Veneer—Least expensive

Vaults

• Regardless of what you pay, no assumptions should be made regarding quality, or ability to protect or delay human decomposition.

• Vaults are primarily made of concrete with many optional features available. Some areas of the country use steel, fiberglass, and plastic, depending upon local suppliers and consumer preference.

• Vaults can vary in quality, price, and ability to protect the casket. Prices should be carefully compared.

Cemetery Selection

• Veterans have cemetery benefits:1-800-827-1000.

• The most important consideration when purchasing a gravesite or a niche in a Columbarium is the financial condition of the cemetery and its continuing ability to maintain the grounds or facilities to meet your standards.

• Do not hesitate to ask about their perpetual care funds. These funds are set aside for the future maintenance of the grounds and facilities.

• Consider all costs before purchasing anything. Remember, it is very difficult to get what you originally paid for cemetery property when reselling.

> Cost of grave

> Opening and closing the grave

Monument or marker

- A monument is above ground level, while a marker is flat. Prices vary considerably and are worth comparing.

Flowers

- Similar to music, flowers are one of the most overlooked options of a memorial service. Many florists simply do not have experience or talent advising families about the use of flowers in conjunction with memorial services. When meeting with the florist, consider the following: Pictures, memorabilia, size of facility, and flower stands available through the florist or the funeral home. By using a competent florist who is interested in working with the aforementioned elements, flowers can add beauty and warmth to the memorial service.

Memorial Announcement

- A memorial announcement can be an appropriate, effective, and inexpensive method to notify a selective group of people that someone has died. Memorial announcements may be personalized to meet each family's needs. It can be very effective for notifying friends and family who live far away. *Take this book with you to a PRINTER and show them exactly what you want, using the enclosed samples of memorial announcements in this guide (see page 149).*

Obituary—

- Your primary option is to have an obituary notice, possibly naming an organization where memorial contributions may be sent. This will allow family and friends to express their sympathy in lieu of memorial services or a funeral (see page 147).

STEP 5

Gather Price Information

- Start by selecting one funeral home as a "guinea pig" for collecting pricing and product information. Later, you will make telephone calls to other funeral homes, casket stores and other related businesses to gather prices for comparison. Select your guinea pig carefully using recommendations from reliable sources such as family, clergy, or business associates. Look for a privately owned funeral home if possible.

  > While at the funeral home, discuss the services you are interested in and any options associated with them. Talk specifically about their services, including assistance after the funeral or memorial if desired and the cost of what you are planning.

  > After you clearly understand what services you are selecting, ask for the price with subtractions made for services you do not desire. Make sure you obtain prices for everything you will need.

  > Remember, the funeral home must give you a price list for their services for you to take home. Make sure you understand it thoroughly and keep it for further price comparison.

  > After you have completed your shopping trip to the guinea pig funeral home and have their prices for their services and other products, your next step is to use the telephone to go comparison-shopping.

  > Try to narrow down your choices of caskets to make comparison-shopping easier.

Casket Shopping Strategy At The Guinea Pig

- Your objective is to find a casket you like, find out what it costs, and how cooperative a particular business is in finding a casket that suits your needs.

- Look at their casket price list and notice which price range has the largest selection of caskets. Usually they will list a few very cheap ones and a few very expensive ones, with the majority somewhere in between.

NOTE—If you don't ask, you could be comparing prices from the same firm, which could lead you to believe that prices must be consistent across the board.

- Funeral homes and casket stores do this to create an average price image in the customer's mind. They also offer the most selection in the price range from which they want you to buy.

- If, for example, you want an inexpensive wooden casket, and there isn't one on the price list, ask to see one. If you are not satisfied with their response, ask to see the manufacturer catalog. Batesville, the largest casket manufacturer, carries close to 100 steel caskets and over 30 wooden caskets.

- If you request a bronze casket, they'll deliver it on Easter Sunday. You should expect the same service if you choose a less expensive wooden or metal casket.

- If your first funeral home selection does not prove to be worthwhile, due to lack of cooperation or willingness to help you, move on.

- Once you have chosen a casket, ask for and write down very carefully the manufacturer, the model number, the model name, and the price. You will need this information later while comparison-shopping by phone.

- Casket names are intentionally changed by funeral homes to avoid comparison-shopping, so be able to describe in detail the casket in which you are interested.

- Using the Telephone Checklist on the next page and the Yellow Page section of your phone book, call at least three funeral homes for price information. When calling, ask each funeral home if they are associated with or co-owned by any other funeral homes in your area. It is common for a conglomerate to own several funeral homes and cemeteries in an area and operate under different names.

- It is required by law in all 50 states that price information be given over the phone.

- Surveys have shown that prices can range considerably in areas with little competition. Don't be hesitant to call for prices in neighboring communities. The savings may be well worth the call.

- If you prefer, visit the funeral homes of choice and request a **General Price List**. *It is required by law that upon request, General Price Lists be given to the public.*

Telephone Checklist

NOTE: It is very important to obtain accurate prices for the services you desire, so request totals. Bait and switch discrepancies may arise during final arrangements if you don't obtain exact price quotes in the beginning.

I would like package price information for immediate burial,
without visitation or services using

_____

(name and description of casket)

and _____

(description of vault)

and _____.

(name of cemetery)

Description of Casket and Vault—Selected at "Guinea Pig" Funeral Home

	Manufacturer	Name	Type	Model
Casket Example:	Batesville	Pacific Pine	pine	Identifying number
Casket Chioice 1.				
Casket Chioice 2.				
Vault Example:	Wilbert	Venetian	basic concrete	N/A
Vault Chioice 1.				
Vault Chioice 2.				

USE FORM ON FOLLOWING PAGE

Telephone Checklist

	Company Example	Company A	Company B	Company C
Funeral Home Name:	Sunset			
Funeral Home Representative:	John Doe			
Date:	9/01/02			
Phone Number:	810-230-0000			
	PRICES	PRICES	PRICES	PRICES
Package Services of Funeral Home, Removal, Transport to Cemetery:	$700*			
Private Family Viewing:	$0*			
Other Services	None chosen			
TOTAL OF SERVICES:	$700*			
Casket:	$575*			
Casket Description (Name):	Batesville Pacific Pine			
Outer Burial Container (Vault):	$300*			
O.B.C. Description (Name):	Wilbert Basic Concrete			
Other:	None chosen			
TOTAL OF MERCHANDISE:	$875*			
TOTAL SERVICES AND MERCHANDISE:	$1,575*			

* The prices above are meant to be merely examples

Additional Expenses—Not Necessary to Compare—Obtain Prices only for Planning Final Cost

Additional Expenses	Example	Price
Cemetery Opening/Closing:	$350*	
Vault Installation:	$75*	
Option of Obituary:	$100*	
Memorial Announcement:	$25*	
Number of Death Certificates (5):	$30*	
Airline Transportation	0*	
Florist:	$75*	
Other:	0*	
SUBTOTAL:	$655*	
Casket—Vault—Burial No Service (total from previous page):	$1,575*	
TOTAL:	$2,230*	

* The prices above are meant to be merely examples

These expenses will primarily be the same for all funeral homes, but knowing their prices will help determine total costs. If these expenses are added into your contract, you may be paying an extra fee, or the funeral home may receive a discount for completing these services.

STEP 6

Comparing Prices and Services

- Compare funeral homes' prices and their willingness to serve you.

- How willing is a funeral home to order a casket or tailor services that meet your needs? If they are not willing, choose another. Funeral directors will bend over backwards if they can take a consumer away from a competitor.

- You do not have to purchase all merchandise and services from one funeral home. Ask for a package discount if you do purchase all services, casket, and vault from the same location.

STEP 7

Finalize Arrangements

NOTE—Final arrangements should be written so that anyone can read and clearly understand the exact services or merchandise purchased. Compare their General Price List with the prices given over the phone. Do this prior to any conversation regarding services or merchandise. If there are any differences or if you are not satisfied, request an explanation. If you are still not satisfied, leave. It may be necessary to report them to the Federal Trade Commission. Funeral Homes are responsible for all employees who quote prices, and can be held accountable.

- Make an appointment to meet with the funeral home of your choice. Take this guide along with the following:

  › Completed obituary form (page 147)—optional

  › Completed death certificate form (page 151)

  › List of options you will use (see Step 3).

  › Casket or merchandise choices.

  › If you need assistance locating clergy, a soloist, or if you have questions regarding death certificates, now is the time to inquire.

STEP 8

The careful approach

- *If you decide to prepay your services, be sure you understand all arrangements and have them in writing.*

- Ask any of the following questions that you feel are necessary:

  > Is my money 100 percent refundable at any time?

  > Can I transfer my arrangements without penalty?

  > Where will my money be placed (bank, savings & loan, insurance, or trust) ?

  > Will I receive a receipt and proof of deposit after payment?

  > What is your commission?

  > What written guarantees do I have that my funds are available when needed?

  > Is my account insured? If yes, by whom?

  > Will I pay taxes on my earned interest?

  > If your funeral home is sold, can I obtain or transfer my money without penalty?

  > Is my money sheltered if I have to go on Medicaid?

  > If you go out of business, what happens to my money?

  > Are you licensed by the state? If yes, please provide proof, including your insurance identification number.

  > If I cancel my arrangements several years from now, who keeps the earned interest?

- If the above questions are not answered to your satisfaction, **do not pay.** If the answers given are not in writing, **do not pay.** If you are pressured, **do not pay.** If you have not compared at least three firms, **do not pay.**

Burial—With Graveside Service

STEP 1   Read the pros and cons of Burial
with Graveside Service

STEP 2   Determine if these arrangements meet the
approval of survivors

STEP 3   Choose options

STEP 4   Detailed description of options

STEP 5   Gather price information

STEP 6   Compare prices, services, and attitudes
of providers

STEP 7   Finalize arrangements

STEP 8   The careful approach

STEP 1

Pros

- Low cost alternative to traditional funerals.

- Provides the same elements valued in funeral services:

    > Gives the opportunity for family and friends to gather.

    > Provides closure and finality.

    > Provides religious ceremony and tradition.

    > Option of open casket for viewing when services are held in a mausoleum at the cemetery

Cons

- The added cost of a casket, vault, grave, and opening and closing grave, versus cremation.

STEP 2

Approval of Survivors

- In a pre-need situation, determine if the arrangements you are making meet the approval of your next of kin or survivors. In some states, survivors can change pre-arrangements after death has occurred. However, arrangements need not be altered if they are discussed and survivors understand your wishes while you are living.

STEP 3

Choosing Options

- Review the following options and decide which ones you will use for the funeral service.

    > Various services of funeral homes

    > Casket selection

    > Outer burial container (vault) selection

> Cemetery selection

> Monument or marker

> Obituary notice

> Memorial announcement

> Flowers

> Having an open or closed casket.

> Use of clergy or speaker

STEP 4

Details of Options   *Funeral Home Services*

- The death of a family member, friend, or loved one will find you in no mood to make multitudes of difficult decisions. If you are responsible for making someone's funeral or memorial services, then pre-thinking your options—not pre-paying—is helpful.

- In Step 5, you will shop for the "best price" and the "best services." It will be difficult to put a dollar value on the compassion and care given to your family, so it is important to take a minute to think about your own situation and the assistance they will need before, during, and after the service.

- In addition to the basic services that all funeral homes offer, there are "additional" services made available by **some** funeral homes. In many cases, these services are the most appreciated functions a funeral home offers because they can make your family's burden more bearable.

- Assistance with Death Certificates: It will be necessary to notify various business and governmental agencies that death has occurred. The following list will help you decide how much assistance you may need to complete these tasks. Many funeral homes offer services for this and can be of invaluable assistance.

  > Real estate transfers

  > Probate court

> Motor vehicles (cars, trucks, boats, etc.)

> Banks, brokers, investments

> Veterans' affairs: 1-800-827-1000

> Social security

> Life insurance

> Pension benefits

- **Some** funeral homes schedule a meeting with the family, providing clerical assistance and transportation to offices or agencies. If you need this service, inquire about the price and decide if the cost is worth the trouble it will save you and your survivors.

- Flower Delivery: Sometimes it is difficult to load all plants, flowers, etc., into your vehicles. Some funeral homes provide this in their professional services fees, while others will charge a separate fee.

- Meals: After the burial, the funeral director should be able to reserve or recommend a place that accommodates funeral or memorial luncheons.

- Hotel Accommodations: The funeral director should be able to recommend a nearby place that is within your budget and suitable to your needs.

- Survivors Workshops: The funeral director should be able to direct you to a group which assists survivors of suicide, sudden infant death, AIDS, etc. Hospitals, church groups, and non-profit organizations often sponsor these activities.

Casket Selection

- Depending upon where you live, there are various options as to where you can buy a casket. Check the Yellow Page section of your telephone directory for any of the following:

> funeral homes

> cemeteries

> retail casket stores

- *Caskets*—Before you attempt to select and compare casket prices, you will need some basic product information. Casket materials greatly affect their cost.

  > Bronze caskets: The most expensive metal casket, usually quite lavish, with high grade velvet interior.

  > Copper caskets: Generally half the price of bronze, but still quite expensive.

  > Steel caskets: Made in three thicknesses:
  > —16-gauge steel—the most lavish and expensive steel casket
  > —18-gauge steel—moderately expensive
  > —20-gauge steel—thinnest, least expensive steel

  > The 20-gauge steel caskets often look cheap, but with flowers, a flag, or pictures on the lid, they do the job.

  > Remember that no casket will preserve or maintain the human body, regardless of what a funeral director or casket manufacturer claims. If such claims are made, ask for proof!

  > Wooden caskets—Price is usually determined by what kind of wood is used and how ornately the interior and exterior are finished.
  > —Walnut or Mahogany—Most expensive
  > —Cherry
  > —Birch, Maple, Oak
  > —Pine
  > —Popple
  > —Veneer—Least expensive

  > Rental Caskets or Ceremonial Caskets—Wooden or metal exteriors with a removable light-weight wood interior and upholstery like traditional caskets. Unfortunately for the consumer, not many funeral homes carry much of a selection, and the casket manufacturers have not done much to promote these economical, practical alternative caskets.

Vaults

> Regardless of what you pay, no assumptions should be made regarding quality, or ability to protect or delay human decomposition.

> Vaults are primarily made of concrete with many optional features available. Some areas of the country use steel, fiberglass, and plastic, depending upon local suppliers and consumer preference.

> Vaults can vary in quality, price, and ability to protect the casket. Prices should be carefully compared.

Cemetery Selection

• The most important consideration when purchasing a gravesite or a niche in a Columbarium is the financial condition of the cemetery and its continuing ability to maintain the grounds or facilities to meet your standards.

> Do not hesitate to ask about their perpetual care funds. These funds are set aside for the future maintenance of the grounds and facilities.

> Consider all costs before purchasing anything. Remember, it is very difficult to get what you originally paid for cemetery property when reselling.
> —Cost of grave
> —Opening and closing the grave

Monument or marker

• A monument is above ground level, while a marker is flat. Prices vary considerably and are worth comparing.

Obituary

• Obituaries can include a wide variety of information useful in notifying friends, family, and business associates. They are especially helpful when they include specific information about visitation times, location, date, time of services, and a listing of charitable organizations where contributions may be sent (see page 147).

Memorial Announcement

- A memorial announcement can be an appropriate, effective, and inexpensive method to notify a selective group of people that someone has died. Memorial announcements may be personalized to meet each family's needs. It can be very effective for notifying friends and family who live far away. *Take this book with you to a PRINTER and show them exactly what you want, using the enclosed samples of memorial announcements in this guide (see page 149).*

Flowers

- Similar to music, flowers are one of the most overlooked options of a memorial service. Many florists simply do not have experience or talent advising families about the use of flowers in conjunction with memorial services. When meeting with the florist, consider the following: Pictures, memorabilia, size of facility, and flower stands available through the florist or the funeral home. By using a competent florist who is interested in working with the aforementioned elements, flowers can add beauty and warmth to the memorial service.

Open or closed casket

- If the deceased has deteriorated in appearance, a framed picture sitting on a closed casket may be the best choice.

Clergy or speaker

- Consider what you want to be said and the desired formality of services **before** choosing your speaker or clergy. **Before** planning too far, check that the person is available. It is very important to give them a few written ideas of what you want to be said and the music to be played. It is highly recommended that you meet this person and make sure that they have a clear understanding of your expectations. If you want an upbeat, uplifting memorial with special music, say so.

STEP 5

**Gather Price
Information**

- Start by selecting one funeral home as a "guinea pig" for collecting pricing and product information. Later, you will make telephone calls to other funeral homes, casket stores and other related businesses to gather prices for comparison. Select your guinea pig carefully using recommendations from reliable sources such as family, clergy, or business associates. Look for a privately owned funeral home if possible.

  > While at the funeral home, discuss the services you are interested in and any options associated with them. Talk specifically about their services, including assistance after the funeral or memorial if desired and the cost of what you are planning.

  > After you clearly understand what services you are selecting, ask for the price with subtractions made for services you do not desire. Make sure you obtain prices for everything you will need.

  > Remember, the funeral home must give you a price list for their services for you to take home. Make sure you understand it thoroughly and keep it for further price comparison.

  > After you have completed your shopping trip to the guinea pig funeral home and have their prices for their services and other products, your next step is to use the telephone to go comparison-shopping.

  > Try to narrow down your choices of caskets to make comparison-shopping easier.

Casket Shopping Strategy

  —Your objective is to find a casket you like, find out what it costs, and how cooperative a particular business is in finding a casket that suits your needs.

  —Look at their casket price list and notice which price range has the largest selection of caskets. Usually they will list a few very cheap ones and a few very expensive ones, with the majority somewhere in between.

- Funeral homes and casket stores do this to create an average price image in the customer's mind. They also offer the most selection in the price range from which they want you to buy.

- If, for example, you want an inexpensive wooden casket, and there isn't one on the price list, ask to see one. If you are not satisfied with their response, ask to see the manufacturer catalog. Batesville, the largest casket manufacturer, carries close to 100 steel caskets and over 30 wooden caskets.

- If you request a bronze casket, they'll deliver it on Easter Sunday. You should expect the same service if you choose a less expensive wooden or metal casket.

- If your first funeral home selection does not prove to be worthwhile, due to lack of cooperation or willingness to help you, move on.

- Once you have chosen a casket, ask for and write down very carefully the manufacturer, the model number, the model name, and the price. You will need this information later while comparison-shopping by phone.

- Casket names are intentionally changed by funeral homes to avoid comparison-shopping, so be able to describe in detail the casket in which you are interested.

NOTE—If you don't ask, you could be comparing prices from the same firm, which could lead you to believe that prices must be consistent across the board.

- Using the Telephone Checklist on the next page and the Yellow Page section of your phone book, call at least three funeral homes for price information. When calling, ask each funeral home if they are associated with or co-owned by any other funeral homes in your area. It is common for a conglomerate to own several funeral homes and cemeteries in an area and operate under different names.

- It is required by law in all 50 states that price information be given over the phone.

- Surveys have shown that prices can range considerably in areas with little competition. Don't be hesitant to call for prices in neighboring communities. The savings may be well worth the call.

- If you prefer, visit the funeral homes of choice and request a **General Price List**. *It is required by law that upon request, General Price Lists be given to the public.*

Vaults

- Before looking at vaults you will receive a vault price list. Once again, you will find a basic vault and a few very expensive ones, with the majority of the selections somewhere in between.

- A vault's primary function is to keep the grave from collapsing, which would cause maintenance problems for the cemetery. Some vaults are also supposed to be "protective." The protective features of a vault are questionable. Consider these points before spending a life's earnings on a protective vault:

  > There is no way to know, aside from digging up the vault, whether or not it is sealed properly.

  > In most Northern climates, the vault lid is not buried beneath the frost line and is subject to freezing and thawing, which can put great pressure on the vault's seal.

  > No vault will preserve the human body. More often vaults trap moisture, creating the problems they claim to prevent.

Telephone Checklist

NOTE: It is very important to obtain accurate prices for the services you desire, so request totals. Bait and switch discrepancies may arise during final arrangements if you don't obtain exact price quotes in the beginning.

I am calling for price information on burial with graveside services held at

_____ ,
(name of cemetery)

using a _____
(description of casket)

and _____ .
(description of vault)

Description of Casket and Vault—Selected at "Guinea Pig" Funeral Home

	Manufacturer	Name	Type	Model
Casket Example:	Batesville	Colonial	pine	Identifying #
Casket Chioice 1.				
Casket Chioice 2.				
Vault Example:	Wilbert	Monticello	basic concrete	N/A
Vault Chioice 1.				
Vault Chioice 2.				

USE FORM ON FOLLOWING PAGE

Telephone Checklist

	Company Example	Company A	Company B	Company C
Funeral Home Name:	Sunset			
Funeral Home Representative:	John Doe			
Date:	9/01/02			
Phone Number:	810-230-0000			
	PRICES	PRICES	PRICES	PRICES
Basic Services of Funeral Director & Staff:	$500*			
Conducting Graveside Services:	$200*			
Embalming (optional):	Not chosen*			
Other preparation:	Not chosen*			
Removal from Place of Death:	$100*			
Transportation to Cemetery:	$100*			
Other Services	None chosen*			
TOTAL OF SERVICES:	$900*			
Casket:	$1,500*			
Casket Name/Description:	Batesville Colonial Pine			
Outer Burial Container (Vault):	$600*			
O.B.C. Name:	Wilbert Monticello			
Other Merchandise:	None chosen*			
TOTAL OF MERCHANDISE:	$2,100*			
TOTAL MERCHANDISE AND SERVICES:	$3,000*			

* The prices above are meant to be merely examples

Additional Expenses—Not Necessary to Compare—Obtain Prices only for Planning Final Cost

Additional Expenses	Example	Price
Cemetery Opening/Closing:	$350*	
Vault Installation:	$75*	
Obituary (optional):	$100*	
Number of Death Certificates (5):	$30*	
Clergy/speaker:	$100*	
Transportation of Deceased—Airline etc.	0*	
Florist:	$75*	
Memorial Announcement:	0*	
SUBTOTAL:	$730*	
Casket/Vault/Graveside Services (total from previous page):	$3,000*	
TOTAL:	$3,730*	

* The prices above are meant to be merely examples

These expenses will primarily be the same for all funeral homes, but knowing their prices will help determine total costs. If these expenses are added into your contract, you may be paying an extra fee, or the funeral home may receive a discount for completing these services.

STEP 6

Compare Prices

- Compare funeral homes' prices and their willingness to serve you.

- How willing is a funeral home to order a casket or vault or tailor services that meet your needs? If they are not willing, choose another. Funeral directors will bend over backwards if they can take a consumer away from a competitor.

- You do not have to purchase all merchandise and services from one funeral home. Ask for a package discount if you do purchase all services, casket, and vault from the same location.

- If you choose to hold the services in a mausoleum at the cemetery, inspect the facilities for cleanliness, adequate parking, and handicap accessibility. Ask to see the area where your service will be held and ask about their ability to assist you with options you have chosen.

STEP 7

Finalize Arrangements and Services

NOTE—Final arrangements should be written so that anyone can read and clearly understand the exact services or merchandise purchased. Compare their General Price List with the prices given over the phone. Do this prior to any conversation regarding services or merchandise. If there are any differences or if you are not satisfied, request an explanation. If you are still not satisfied, leave. It may be necessary to report them to the Federal Trade Commission. Funeral Homes are responsible for all employees who quote prices, and can be held accountable.

- Make an appointment to meet with the funeral home of your choice. Take this guide along with the following:

  > Completed obituary form (page 147)—optional

  > Completed death certificate form (page 151).

  > List of options you will use (see Step 3).

  > Casket selection (page 116).

  > Vault selection (page 116).

  > If you need assistance locating a clergy, soloist, or have questions regarding death certificates, now is the time to inquire.

STEP 8

The Careful Approach

- *If you decide to prepay your services, be sure you understand all arrangements and have them in writing.*

- Ask any of the following questions that you feel are necessary:

  > Is my money 100 percent refundable at any time?

  > Can I transfer my arrangements without penalty?

  > Where will my money be placed (bank, savings & loan, insurance, or trust) ?

  > Will I receive a receipt and proof of deposit after payment?

  > What is your commission?

  > What written guarantees do I have that my funds are available when needed?

  > Is my account insured? If yes, by whom?

  > Will I pay taxes on my earned interest?

  > If your funeral home is sold, can I obtain or transfer my money without penalty?

  > Is my money sheltered if I have to go on Medicaid?

  > If you go out of business, what happens to my money?

  > Are you licensed by the state? If yes, please provide proof, including your insurance identification number.

  > If I cancel my arrangements several years from now, who keeps the earned interest?

- If the above questions are not answered to your satisfaction, **do not pay.** If the answers given are not in writing, **do not pay.** If you are pressured, **do not pay.** If you have not compared at least three firms, **do not pay.**

Burial—With Funeral Service

STEP 1   Read the pros and cons of Burial
          with Funeral Service

STEP 2   Determine if these arrangements meet the
          approval of survivors

STEP 3   Choose options

STEP 4   Detailed description of options

STEP 5   Gather price information

STEP 6   Compare prices, services, and attitudes
          of providers

STEP 7   Finalize arrangements

STEP 8   The careful approach

STEP 1

Pros

- Provides all of the alternatives and options possible in funeral services.

- Allows family and friends the opportunity to view the deceased, participate in the funeral process and provides a sense of closure or finality.

Cons

- Most expensive method of funeral ritual.

- The added cost of a casket, vault, grave, and opening and closing grave, versus cremation.

STEP 2

Approval of Survivors

- In a pre-need situation, determine if the arrangements you are making meet the approval of your next of kin or survivors. In some states, survivors can change pre-arrangements after death has occurred. However, arrangements need not be altered if they are discussed and survivors understand your wishes while you are living.

STEP 3

Choosing Options

- Review the following options and decide which ones you will use for the funeral service.

  > Various services offered by funeral home.

  > Casket selection

  > Vault selection

  > Cemetery selection

  > Monument or marker

> Flowers

> Memorial announcement

> Obituary

> Having an open or closed casket

> Use of clergy or speaker

> Date and time

> Location of funeral

> Number of people attending

> Music

> Private or public services

> Funeral accessories

> Luncheon following funeral service

> Pictures and memorabilia

> Visitation times before funeral

> Military committal services

> Fraternal organization services

> Greeters or Ushers

STEP 4

Detailed Description of Options

Funeral Home Services

- The death of a family member, friend, or loved one will find you in no mood to make multitudes of difficult decisions. If you are responsible for making someone's funeral or memorial services, then pre-thinking your options—not pre-paying—is helpful.

- In Step 5, you will shop for the "best price" and the "best services." It will be difficult to put a dollar value on the compassion and care given to your family, so it is important to take a minute to think about your own situation and the assistance they will need before, during, and after the service.

- In addition to the basic services that all funeral homes offer, there are "additional" services made available by **some** funeral homes. In many cases, these services are the most appreciated functions a funeral home offers because they can make your family's burden more bearable.

- Assistance with Death Certificates: It will be necessary to notify various business and governmental agencies that death has occurred. The following list will help you decide how much assistance you may need to complete these tasks. Many funeral homes offer services for this and can be of invaluable assistance.

    > Real estate transfers

    > Probate court

    > Motor vehicles (cars, trucks, boats, etc.)

    > Banks, brokers, investments

    > Veterans' affairs

    > Social security

    > Life insurance

    > Pension benefits

- **Some** funeral homes schedule a meeting with the family, providing clerical assistance and transportation to offices or agencies. If you need this service, inquire about the price and decide if the cost is worth the trouble it will save you and your survivors.

- Flower Delivery: Sometimes it is difficult to load all plants, flowers, etc., into your vehicles. Some funeral homes provide this in their professional services fees, while others will charge a separate fee.

- Meals: After the burial, the funeral director should be able to reserve or recommend a place that accommodates funeral or memorial luncheons.

- Hotel Accommodations: The funeral director should be able to recommend a nearby place that is within your budget and suitable to your needs.

- Survivors Workshops: The funeral director should be able to direct you to a group which assists survivors of suicide, sudden infant death, AIDS, etc. Hospitals, church groups, and non-profit organizations often sponsor these activities.

Casket Selection

- Depending upon where you live, there are various options as to where you can buy a casket. Check the Yellow Page section of your telephone directory for any of the following:

  > funeral homes

  > cemeteries

  > retail casket stores

- *Caskets*—Before you attempt to select and compare casket prices, you will need some basic product information. Casket materials greatly affect their cost.

  > Bronze caskets: The most expensive metal casket, usually quite lavish, with high grade velvet interior.

  > Copper caskets: Generally half the price of bronze, but still quite expensive.

  > Steel caskets: Made in three thicknesses:
  >> —16-gauge steel—the most lavish and expensive steel casket
  >> —18-gauge steel—moderately expensive
  >> —20-gauge steel—thinnest, least expensive steel

  > The 20-gauge steel caskets often look cheap, but with flowers, a flag, or pictures on the lid, they do the job.

  > Remember that no casket will preserve or maintain the human body, regardless of what a funeral director or casket manufacturer claims. If such claims are made, ask for proof!

  > Wooden caskets—Price is usually determined by what kind of wood is used and how ornately the interior and exterior are finished.
  >> —Walnut or Mahogany—Most expensive
  >> —Cherry

WARNINGS—
- Compare prices carefully. Prices vary based on workmanship and materials.
- When pre-purchasing ask for a guarantee **in writing** that you will get your money or merchandise back if that business fails.
- Casket designs and models do change with time. Ask for a guarantee **in writing** that you will receive the manufacturer and the quality you have chosen.
- Some funeral homes offer "packages" that allow for "discounts" when all merchandise and services are purchased from them. Ask about these package deals.
- Prices can vary hundreds of dollars between dealers for the same merchandise.

—Birch, Maple, Oak

—Pine

—Poplar

—Veneer—Least expensive

> Rental Caskets or Ceremonial Caskets—Wooden or metal exteriors with a removable lightweight wood interior and upholstery like traditional caskets. Unfortunately for the consumer, not many funeral homes carry much of a selection, and the casket manufacturers have not done much to promote these economical, practical alternative caskets.

Vaults

• Regardless of what you pay, no assumptions should be made regarding quality, or ability to protect or delay human decomposition.

• Vaults are primarily made of concrete with many optional features available. Some areas of the country use steel, fiberglass, and plastic, depending upon local suppliers and consumer preference.

• Vaults can vary in quality, price, and ability to protect the casket. Prices should be carefully compared.

Cemetery Selection

• The most important consideration when purchasing a gravesite or a niche in a Columbarium is the financial condition of the cemetery and its continuing ability to maintain the grounds or facilities to meet your standards.

• Do not hesitate to ask about their perpetual care funds. These funds are set aside for the future maintenance of the grounds and facilities.

• Consider all costs before purchasing anything. Remember, it is very difficult to get what you originally paid for cemetery property when reselling.

> Cost of grave

> Opening and closing the grave

Monument or marker

- A monument is above ground level, while a marker is flat. Prices vary considerably and are worth comparing.

Flowers

- Similar to music, flowers are one of the most overlooked options of a memorial service. Many florists simply do not have experience or talent advising families about the use of flowers in conjunction with memorial services. When meeting with the florist, consider the following: Pictures, memorabilia, size of facility, and flower stands available through the florist or the funeral home. By using a competent florist who is interested in working with the aforementioned elements, flowers can add beauty and warmth to the memorial service.

Memorial Announcement

- A memorial announcement can be an appropriate, effective, and inexpensive method to notify a selective group of people that someone has died. Memorial announcements may be personalized to meet each family's needs. It can be very effective for notifying friends and family who live far away. *Take this book with you to a PRINTER and show them exactly what you want, using the enclosed samples of memorial announcements in this guide (see page 149).*

Obituary

- Obituaries can include a wide variety of information useful in notifying friends, family, and business associates. They are especially helpful when they include specific information about visitation times, location, date, time of services, and a listing of charitable organizations where contributions may be sent (see page 147).

Open or closed casket

- If the deceased has deteriorated in appearance, a framed picture sitting on a closed casket may be the best choice.

Clergy or Speaker

- Consider what you want to be said and the desired formality of services **before** choosing your speaker or clergy. **Before** planning too far, check that the person is available. It is very important to give them a few written ideas of what you want to be said and the music to be played. It is highly recommended that you meet this person and make sure that they have a clear understanding of your expectations. If you want an upbeat, uplifting memorial with special music, say so.

Date and Time

- Before you set a date and time, make sure all facilities, people involved (family from out of town), clergy, luncheon facility, flower shop, etc., can accommodate or attend on that date and at that time. A few quick calls can prevent changing plans at the last minute.

Location of Funeral

- Churches and funeral homes are common locations for funeral services. However, funerals can be held anywhere people can gather, considering seating capacity, parking, time of year, and availability.

- *Even if you are not a member, many churches will allow you to use their facility for a reasonable fee*—usually for much less than the cost of using a funeral home's facilities. Many churches have sound systems, plenty of seating, parking, and a place for a luncheon following the services.

Number of People

- Factors that determine the number of people attending a funeral service could be the age of the deceased, social and church involvement, achievements, and whether or not an obituary was placed in the paper. The reasons for needing to know approximately how many people will attend:

  > Number of memorial folders (optional)

  > Size and location of facility to be used

> Number of people for luncheon (optional)

> Assistance needed at funeral service

Music

- Music is often the most overlooked and under-utilized aspect of a funeral service. It can be very comforting and uplifting to use music in conjunction with the spoken message. By using "personal favorite" selections, whether they are traditional hymns, modern music, contemporary, jazz, country, rock, or spiritual, you will be adding beauty and meaning to the service. With some planning, such accompaniments as piano, violin, bagpipes, guitar, flute, or a soloist singing a favorite song can add a great deal to services that have traditionally been limited to traditional hymns.

- Some creative and memorable musical selections requested by families for funerals have been: "Take Me Out To The Ball Game"; "My Way," by Frank Sinatra; "Somewhere Over The Rainbow," by Judy Garland; "Danny Boy," by Kate Smith; "Stairway To Heaven," by Led Zeppelin (used for a teenager killed in an auto accident); "Amazing Grace" (played on bagpipes); "Unforgettable," by Nat King Cole; "Evergreen," by Barbara Streisand; "Ave Maria," by Pavarotti; "Bridge Over Troubled Water," by Simon and Garfunkel; "Desperado," by The Eagles and "The National Anthem," by Arthur Fiedler and the Boston Philharmonic (Veterans Service).

- Most churches and funeral homes have the necessary sound equipment to play cassettes or compact discs, and given enough time, can arrange for musicians. If you are having services at an "alternative" site and would like a musician, call a church, college/university or an institute of music for a referral.

Private or Public Memorial Services

- Sometimes immediate friends and families can be more comforting than hoards of people you may not know, or may not care to see at that time. If you opt for a private funeral service, mention it in the obituary or do not run an obituary until after the service is held.

Funeral Accessories

- Memorial Folders: Memorial folders are traditionally used for Protestant services, and are available through funeral homes, some church supply stores, and printers. Their purpose is debatable, since most end up left on church pews or folded up in a pocket, later to be discarded.

- Prayer Cards: Prayer cards are traditionally used for Catholic and Orthodox faiths and are available through funeral homes, some church supply stores, and printers.

- Register Books: Register books are especially helpful if they have name and address lines to aid in sending "thank-you" notes, if so desired. Register books are frequently sold at funeral homes for $25.00 to $65.00, and similar products are available for much less through stationary and church supply stores.

- Thank-you Notes: Thank-you notes are usually sent to those that pay a special kindness to you such as sending flowers, making memorial contributions to charitable organizations, assisting in funeral services, and providing food for a luncheon. They are available at funeral homes, stationary stores, and card shops. It is usually worth shopping around; sometimes selections offered at funeral homes are limited and expensive.

Luncheon

- Serving lunch after a funeral is sometimes quite nice, whether you serve coffee and pastry or a multi-course meal provided by a top-notch restaurant or caterer. Luncheons offer a chance for friends to talk and families to come together, which may begin the process of healing.

Use of Pictures, Videos, or Memorabilia

- Pictures taken throughout a person's life can be very important and meaningful in terms of comforting a family. You can use pictures, photographs, and videos to remember a person when they were happy, successful, content, in love, proud; the list is endless. Such pictures can be more meaningful than viewing a body which, due to injury or illness, is not what you care to remember.

Visitation

- Consider allowing a period of time before or after the service to visit with friends and family. If you are having an obituary printed, it is suggested that such times be listed.

Military Services

- If a person served during a time of war and was honorably discharged from the military, he or she should be entitled to military services. The local Veterans of Foreign Wars organization (V.F.W.) can usually arrange for a graveside service including a chaplain, bugler, honor guard, and gun salute.

Fraternal/Religious Organization Services

- There are too many to list, but if a person had a strong affiliation with such organizations as the Masons, Demolay, or Knights of Columbus, they will quite often have a memorial service at the funeral home the evening before the funeral service if you so choose.

Greeters/Ushers

- Greeters and ushers can be members of the family or close friends who are willing to help greet people, hang coats, ask visitors to sign the register book, and hand out memorial folders or prayer cards.

STEP 5

Gather Price Information

- Start by selecting one funeral home as a "guinea pig" for collecting pricing and product information. Later, you will make telephone calls to other funeral homes, casket stores and other related businesses to gather prices for comparison. Select your guinea pig carefully using recommendations from reliable sources such as family, clergy, or business associates. Look for a privately owned funeral home if possible.

> While at the funeral home, discuss the services you are interested in and any options associated with them. Talk specifically about their services, including assistance after the funeral or memorial if desired and the cost of what you are planning.

> After you clearly understand what services you are selecting, ask for the price with subtractions made for services you do not desire. Make sure you obtain prices for everything you will need.

> Remember, the funeral home must give you a price list for their services for you to take home. Make sure you understand it thoroughly and keep it for further price comparison.

> After you have completed your shopping trip to the guinea pig funeral home and have their prices for their services and other products, your next step is to use the telephone to go comparison-shopping.

> Try to narrow down your choices of caskets to make comparison-shopping easier.

Casket Shopping Strategy At the Guinea Pig

- Your objective is to find a casket you like, find out what it costs, and how cooperative a particular business is in finding a casket that suits your needs.

- Look at their casket price list and notice which price range has the largest selection of caskets. Usually they will list a few very cheap ones and a few very expensive ones, with the majority somewhere in between.

- Funeral homes and casket stores do this to create an average price image in the customer's mind. They also offer the most selection in the price range from which they want you to buy.

- If, for example, you want an inexpensive wooden casket, and there isn't one on the price list, ask to see one. If you are not satisfied with their response, ask to see the manufacturer catalog. Batesville, the largest casket manufacturer, carries close to 100 steel caskets and over 30 wooden caskets.

- If you request a bronze casket, they'll deliver it on Easter Sunday. You should expect the same service if you choose a less expensive wooden or metal casket.

- If your first funeral home selection does not prove to be worthwhile, due to lack of cooperation or willingness to help you, move on.

- Once you have chosen a casket, ask for and write down very carefully the manufacturer, the model number, the model name, and the price. You will need this information later while comparison-shopping by phone.

- Casket names are intentionally changed by funeral homes to avoid comparison-shopping, so be able to describe in detail the casket in which you are interested.

NOTE—If you don't ask, you could be comparing prices from the same firm, which could lead you to believe that prices must be consistent across the board.

- Using the Telephone Checklist on the next page and the Yellow Page section of your phone book, call at least three funeral homes for price information. When calling, ask each funeral home if they are associated with or co-owned by any other funeral homes in your area. It is common for a conglomerate to own several funeral homes and cemeteries in an area and operate under different names.

- It is required by law in all 50 states that price information be given over the phone.

- Surveys have shown that prices can range considerably in areas with little competition. Don't be hesitant to call for prices in neighboring communities. The savings may be well worth the call.

- If you prefer, visit the funeral homes of choice and request a **General Price List**. *It is required by law that upon request, General Price Lists be given to the public.*

Vaults

- Before looking at vaults you will receive a vault price list. Once again, you will find a basic vault and a few very expensive ones, with the majority of the selections somewhere in between.

- A vault's primary function is to keep the grave from collapsing, which would cause maintenance problems for the cemetery. Some vaults are also supposed to be "protective." The protective features of a vault are questionable. Consider these points before spending a life's earnings on a protective vault:

  > There is no way to know, aside from digging up the vault, whether or not it is sealed properly.

  > In most Northern climates, the vault lid is not buried beneath the frost line and is subject to freezing and thawing, which can put great pressure on the vault's seal.

  > No vault will preserve the human body. More often vaults trap moisture, creating the problems they claim to prevent.

Telephone Checklist

NOTE: It is very important to obtain accurate prices for the services you desire, so request totals. Bait and switch discrepancies may arise during final arrangements if you don't obtain exact price quotes in the beginning.

I am calling for price information on funeral services held at

_____ ,

(name of funeral home or church)

using _____ and _____

(description of casket)   (description of vault)

with burial in _____.

(name of cemetery)

I would also like price information on (draw a line through those you are not using):

_____ days of visitation, embalming, and _____ limousines from the funeral home to cemetery.

(1/2 day, 1 day, 2 days)   (#)

Description of Casket and Vault—Selected at "Guinea Pig" Funeral Home

	Manufacturer	Name	Type	Model
Casket Example:	Batesville	Casket Name	solid maple	Identifying number
Casket Chioice 1.				
Casket Chioice 2.				
Vault Example:	Wilbert	Venetian	basic concrete	N/A
Vault Chioice 1.				
Vault Chioice 2.				

Telephone Checklist

	Company Example	Company A	Company B	Company C
Funeral Home Name:	Sunset			
Funeral Home Representative:	John Doe			
Date:	9/01/02			
Phone Number:	810-230-0000			
	PRICES	PRICES	PRICES	PRICES
Basic Services of Funeral Director & Staff:	$500*			
Conducting Funeral Ceremony (church or chapel:	$300*			
Embalming:	$300*			
Other Preparation:	$100*			
Use of Facilities	$150*			
Removal from Place of Death:	$100*			
Hearse to Cemetery:	$100*			
Limousines _____#:	$100*			
Other Services:	None chosen*			
TOTAL OF SERVICES:	$1,650*			
Casket:	$2.232*			
Casket Description:	Batesville Solid Maple			
Vault:	$800*			
Vault Description:	Wilbert Venetian			
Register Book:	$25*			
Service Folder/Prayer Cards:	$25*			
Thank You Notes:	$15*			
Other:				
TOTAL OF MERCHANDISE:	$3,097*			
TOTAL OF MERCHANDISE & SERVICES:	$4,747*			

* The prices above are meant to be merely examples

Additional Expenses—Not Necessary to Compare—Obtain Prices only for Planning Final Cost

Additional Expenses	Example	Price
Cemetery Opening/Closing:	$350*	
Vault Installation:	$75*	
Obituary:	$100*	
Number of Death Certificates (5):	$30*	
Clergy/church:	$100*	
Musicians/organist/soloist	$100*	
Hair preparation:	$40*	
Luncheon:		
Memorial Announcement:	$25*	
Permits:	0*	
Transportation of Deceased—Airline etc.:	0*	
Florist:	$200*	
TOTAL ADDITIONAL EXPENSES:	$1,020*	
TOTAL PREVIOUS PAGE:	$4,747*	
TOTAL:	$5,767*	

* The prices above are meant to be merely examples

These expenses will primarily be the same for all funeral homes, but knowing their prices will help determine total costs. If these expenses are added into your contract, you may be paying an extra fee, or the funeral home may re-

STEP 6

Compare Prices and Services

- Compare funeral homes' prices and their willingness to serve you.

- How willing is a funeral home to order a casket or tailor services that meet your needs? If they are not willing, choose another. Funeral directors will bend over backwards if they can take a consumer away from a competitor.

- You do not have to purchase all merchandise and services from one funeral home. Ask for a package discount if you do purchase all services, casket, and vault from the same location.

- Inspect facilities for cleanliness, adequate parking, and handicap accessibility. Ask to see the area where your service will be held and ask about their ability to assist you with music selections or other options you have chosen.

STEP 7

Finalize Arrangements

NOTE—Final arrangements should be written so that anyone can read and clearly understand the exact services or merchandise purchased. Compare their General Price List with the prices given over the phone. Do this prior to any conversation regarding services or merchandise. If there are any differences or if you are not satisfied, request an explanation. If you are still not satisfied, leave. It may be necessary to report them to the Federal Trade Commission. Funeral Homes are responsible for all employees who quote prices, and can be held accountable.

- Make an appointment to meet with the funeral home of your choice. Take this guide along with the following:

  > Completed obituary form (page 147)—optional

  > Completed death certificate form (page 151).

  > List of options you will use (see Step 3).

  > Casket selection (page 136).

  > Vault selection (page 136).

  > If you need assistance locating a clergy, soloist, or have questions regarding death certificates, now is the time to inquire.

STEP 8

The Careful Approach

- *If you decide to prepay your services, be sure you understand all arrangements and have them in writing.*

- Ask any of the following questions that you feel are necessary:

  > Is my money 100 percent refundable at any time?

  > Can I transfer my arrangements without penalty?

  > Where will my money be placed (bank, savings & loan, insurance, or trust)?

  > Will I receive a receipt and proof of deposit after payment?

  > What is your commission?

  > What written guarantees do I have that my funds are available when needed?

  > Is my account insured? If yes, by whom?

  > Will I pay taxes on my earned interest?

  > If your funeral home is sold, can I obtain or transfer my money without penalty?

  > Is my money sheltered if I have to go on Medicaid?

  > If you go out of business, what happens to my money?

  > Are you licensed by the state? If yes, please provide proof, including your insurance identification number.

  > If I cancel my arrangements several years from now, who keeps the earned interest?

- If the above questions are not answered to your satisfaction, **do not pay.** If the answers given are not in writing, **do not pay.** If you are pressured, **do not pay.** If you have not compared at least three firms, **do not pay.**

PART 3

References

Vital Records

Use the space here to keep track of information you will need for the funeral planning process and for the administrative tasks that follow. If you are pre-planning your own funeral, providing the information listed in this chapter will save your heirs a ton of work.

Immediately After Death—Before the Funeral: People to Contact—Places to Look—Things to do

(Include phone numbers, addresses, and any guidance or suggestions that may help your survivors.)

Personal Representative: _____

Family Members (in order of calling preference):

_____

_____

_____

_____

_____

_____

_____

_____

_____

_____

Funeral Home or Memorial Society: _____

_____

Clergy—Church: _____

_____

Banks: _____

_____

_____

Stockbroker: _____

_____

Attorney—Location of will: _____

Financial Advisor: _____

Business Associates: _____

_____

_____

_____

_____

_____

Location of Safe Deposit Box, Key, and Contact Person:

_____

_____

Employer, Personnel Department Representative:

_____

Life Insurance Agent: _____

_____

Pallbearers, if needed: _____

_____

_____

_____

_____

_____

Veteran of Foreign Wars—Post and Commander (Especially if you are having a military service):

_____

_____

_____

Fraternal or Religious Organization (Especially if they are doing a memorial service):

_____

_____

_____

Final Arrangements

Location of pre-arrangement contracts, paid statements, insurance, or federal fund:

_____

_____

_____

_____

_____

_____

_____

_____

Burial:

Funeral Home or Memorial Society Name

_____

Address _____

City _____

State _____

Phone Number(s)_____

_____

Body Donation:

University or Institution for Body Donation

_____

Address _____

City _____

State _____

Contact Person: _____

Phone Number(s)_____

_____

Cremation:

Funeral Home, Cemetery or Crematory

_____

Address _____

City _____

State _____

Phone Number(s) _____

Obituary Form

Obituary Information

With a little thought, time, and effort, obituaries can be a touching tribute. You will have to pay a fee to most newspapers to publish an obituary. Usually the fee is based on the length of the obituary. There may be an additional fee if they print a picture of the deceased.

Obituaries are not required by law in any state, and you do not have to pay a funeral director to write one.

Your local newspaper will gladly quote a price, if you give them a written copy in advance. They may give you a format to follow, or they may allow you to use the format of your choice.

It may be a good idea to place an obituary in a paper published where the deceased was raised, especially if there are still family and friends living in that area.

You can use the following list to help you begin writing an obituary—pick and choose applicable items:

Name: _____

Nickname: _____

Date of birth: _____

Date of death: _____

Place of birth: _____

Place of death: _____

Place of residence: _____

Education: _____

_____

Proud accomplishments: _____

_____

_____

_____

_____

Hobbies: _____

Religious affiliations: _____

Military background: _____

Name and address where memorial contributions may be sent:

_____

_____

Memberships: _____

_____

_____

Time, date, location of funeral or memorial: _____

_____

Visitation times: _____

_____

Special anniversaries or milestones: _____

_____

_____

_____

"Survived by" (list surviving family members or companions—perhaps close friends):

_____

_____

_____

_____

Preceded in death by" (list immediate family members or companions who are deceased):

_____

_____

_____

Memorial Announcement Sample

INSERT PHOTOGRAPH HERE

In Loving Memory of
Pamela Sue Beck

Front Cover—Usually a picture of the person.

Pamela Sue Beck, age 91, born June 4, died January 16, 2002. Funeral Services were held January 18, at St. John the Baptist Church in Curran, Michigan, the Reverend Waylon Smolinski officiating. Memorial Contributions may be made to the Alcona County Library. She was born in Glennie, Michigan to Dan and Marlene Johnston and was a resident of the Curran area most of her life. She married Jeff Beck August 17, 1935 at the Curran Baptist Church. She was a charter member of the American Business Women's Association and a member of Ducks Unlimited. She will be remembered as a loving mother and grandmother that brought her family together with love, humor, and good duck calling. She is survived by two daughters: Nina and husband Houston Beanmore, of Santa Barbara, California, and Taylor and Jerry Trost of Posen, Michigan.

Inside Front—Usually obituary information.

Leave blank so you can write a short note to friends, family, and business-work associates.

Inside Right

Memorial announcements are an inexpensive and thoughtful way to remember the ones we love and notify friends and family of a death. They are typically sent to those who cannot attend services, or as a memorial when services are not held.

Take a photograph and obituary information, along with any other information you would like included to your local printer, and he or she can customize an announcement to suit your needs. They can be made as large or small as the family so chooses.

Death Certificate Information Worksheet

The required information varies depending on the state in which you live. Contact your local health department, county clerk, or funeral home for the information your state requires.

Certified copies of the death certificate are issued by the county in which you die. They are recorded with the State Health Department, in the state in which you die.

Certified copies of the death certificate are needed for:

- Passing title of property
- Collecting insurance benefits
- Probate Court
- Collecting pension benefits for survivors
- Stocks
- Bank accounts
- Secretary of State or Department of Motor Vehicles
- Social Security benefits
- Veterans benefits
- To remove the deceased's name from jointly owned property (even if you decide not to sell the property immediately).

Some funeral homes offer extensive services to assist families with the various governmental agencies and businesses, which require a death certificate. This service may include a representative from the funeral home making appointments as required, or completing and mailing the paperwork needed to meet these requirements.

At the time of death, the funeral director will gather the necessary information from survivors to begin the process. The death certificate is then taken to the physician who will be responsible for signing the cause or causes of death. The funeral director will then return it to the county offices for filing. To obtain certified copies, you can go directly to the county in which the person died or contact the funeral director, who may charge a fee for obtaining them for you.

The following page lists the most asked-for information on a death certificate.

NOTE: This information is required for everyone that dies. This can be a tough job, emotionally—go ahead and fill out the blanks as well as you can and get it behind you.

DECEASED'S NAME

First _____

Middle _____

Last _____

Sex   M   F

Date of death: Month/_____Day/_____Year _____

Date of birth: Month/_____Day/_____Year _____

Age _____

County of Death: _____

Location of Death (place officially pronounced dead—hospital or institution):

_____

_____

(If at a hospital: inpatient, operating room, emergency room, dead on arrival [D.O.A.])

City, village, or township:_____

Social Security Number: _____

Occupation (type of work during majority of life): _____

Kind of business or industry: _____

CURRENT RESIDENCE:

Street address: _____

City, village, or township:_____

State: _____

Zip code: _____

Birthplace: _____

City, State, or Foreign Country _____

Marital Status: Married   Never Married   Widowed   Divorced

Surviving Spouse:_____

Served in Military   Yes   No

Ancestry (specify): _____

Race:_____

Education (last grade completed or years of college): _____

Father's First, Middle, Last Name:_____

Mother's First, Middle, Last Name: _____

Method of Disposition: Burial   Cremation   Body Donation

Place of Disposition: _____

Name of Cemetery: _____

Crematory: _____

University of Donation:_____

Location: _____

City or Village: _____

State: _____

Name of Responsible Funeral Director: _____

_____

Many Ways to Save $100s to $1,000s of Dollars

Burial

Caskets

- Comparison shop for caskets, vaults, services of funeral directors, grave markers, and cemeteries. Start by using the yellow pages in your phone book and look under the necessary titles. Call the businesses listed and keep track of the quoted prices on the forms provided in this book. If you have access to the Internet, look under the search term of "caskets." Be careful to compare prices and merchandise carefully, and always consider the cost of shipping, time required to deliver, and the reputation of the business.

- Inexpensive caskets can be dressed up using flowers or a flag if the person was a veteran, or a pall if the person is Roman Catholic.

- Though rental caskets are available to all funeral homes, not all carry them. The outside "shell" is made of wood or metal; the inside container is either buried or cremated. These also amount to a considerable saving of natural resources.

- Some people choose to build their own casket. Plans are available through www.rockler.com or 1-800-279-4441. Allow plenty of time if you are considering this option.

- Inexpensive metal caskets come in a variety of colors and designs. 20 gauge steel caskets come in virtually every color imaginable, but you will be shown a very limited number. Sellers show the most casket choices in the price range they want to sell. Request what you want. Remember, most sellers mark up their merchandise two to three times their cost.

- Inexpensive wood caskets also come in a variety of choices. Batesville Casket Company makes a line of "cremation" caskets that are inexpensive, but these are usually shown only to "cremation clients" to entice them into something with more profit than just cremation.

  > Wood caskets made of veneer are available, but these are not often shown to consumers so as to not take away from more lucrative sales of lavish wood caskets.

  > Caskets made of pine and poplar are sometimes dressed up and marked up when a family is really looking for a plain wood casket

  > Plain wood caskets are available; ask for them. If the funeral home doesn't cooperate, leave.

- If you are looking for an inexpensive casket, and the funeral director sells Batesville Caskets, ask to see the manufacturer's catalog of Batesville cremation caskets. The least expensive caskets are rarely shown to burial customers, but are shown to cremation customers who traditionally don't spend much.

Vaults

- Basic concrete boxes satisfy all requirements at cemeteries, but frequently are not offered by these cemeteries or funeral homes unless requested. Their prices are sometimes elevated even more than other vaults to discourage their use. Compare prices.

- If you are purchasing a "protective" vault, request that it is sealed above ground. The least expensive "protective" vault is usually the best value.

Services

- Consider simple graveside services only, held at the cemetery either at the gravesite or in their chapel, if they have one. Most cemeteries can provide a large tent and chairs (6 or so) for a short outdoor service. Consider the weather and the attendees' ability to stand for the length of the service planned.

- Limit the number of visitation days to only those days that are absolutely necessary. Most funeral homes charge a per day fee for use of their facilities. Delay visitation times until family and friends can arrive.

- Use your church for visitation and services. **Consult with your clergy before making any plans.** Most churches have the perfect facilities for viewing and services, and with a little planning and scheduling, you can eliminate the charges for use of the funeral home facilities. Most churches even have enough members to help the family greet visitors and coordinate services, therefore eliminating the funeral home's charge for conducting the services (primarily the seating of friends and family, the order of the service, and the dismissal of attendees.) You would contact the funeral home for services of removal, embalming, dressing, and cosmetics, transportation to the church and then to the cemetery, and their professional fees. This can usually save the family a significant amount of money.

- Consider cremation or body donation to a university if the costs of a burial are prohibitive. Either option can be followed by a memorial service.

Other

- Ask for package pricing discounts when purchasing all services and merchandise from one provider.

- When ordering flowers, ask the florist which flowers are in season or for any specials they may have.

- Remember to check with Social Security, Veterans, and collect all benefits and insurance monies due. There are services that help locate insurance policies that are lost or stolen.

- Remember that protective caskets and vaults do not stop the deterioration and decomposition of the human body. Millions of dollars are spent yearly on merchandise that does not protect nor preserve as implied.

- Veterans usially receive a small burial allowance, flag, marker, and a grave in a national cemetery. Inquire about benefits.

- Social Security pays a small death benefit but usually only to a surviving spouse.

Cemetery

- Some rural or country cemeteries have much lower fees for the cost of the grave and the costs of opening and closing the grave.

- Consider a flat-ground level grave marker instead of an upright. Before ordering any marker get the rules from the cemetery on what they require. Veterans are given a bronze marker if they were honorably discharged.

- You can save lots of money by buying cemetery property from individuals that no longer have need for them.

Cremation

Cremation Services

- Shop carefully for the best prices. Call funeral homes, cemeteries, and crematories. The included forms will help you keep track of the prices quoted.

- Nonprofit consumer groups may have done the shopping for you. Check their web site at: www.funerals.org.

- Memorial services can be held at various other locations rather than a funeral home. See the list in this book.

- Plan, organize, and direct memorial services without the assistance of a funeral director. See the enclosed organizer and the lists that follow.

- Consider donating the deceased to a local university for anatomical study. Each university has its own policies, so contact them prior to need. Some even pay for removal and transportation of the deceased. Cremation will follow when they are finished.

- Scatter the ashes at your favorite place, instead of burying them at a cemetery or placing them in a niche at a columbarium. Some localities prohibit this, but little is done to enforce it if individuals are discreet in their actions. Consider having a bagpipe player or other musician perform and a few words said, whether religious or not, when burying or scattering ashes. With a little imagination and effort, a memorable, meaningful, and valuable service can be provided to the living for a minimal amount of money.

Urns

- Before you buy an urn, consider what you will do with the ashes. The ashes are usually returned to the family in a plastic box. This box is suitable for burial or keeping the ashes until you scatter them.

- Instead of buying an expensive urn, consider buying a vase that has a lid that can be secured or sealed. After cremation, the ashes can be put in a small plastic bag that can be placed inside your vase, in case you drop it. Whoever does the cremation will put the ashes in the container or urn.

Other

- Ask your florist to arrange flowers around the urn and any special pictures or memorabilia that are being used in the memorial service. If given all of the elements, the florist can design the setting to suit your needs.

- If you decide to view the deceased before cremation, consider a rental casket or a simple inexpensive cremation casket. If the funeral home requests that someone identify the deceased before cremation, request that it be done there on the dressing table or preparation table. A casket should not be required for this purpose.

- If you 're having memorial services, shop around for the best prices on register books, memorial folders, and Thank You cards. Funeral homes usually have a higher markup on these items.

Ideas on Gathering Information for a Meaningful, Memorable, Valuable Service to the Living.

SUGGESTIONS	NOTES
1 Date of birth	
2 Parents/grandparents/family	
3 Schools attended	
4 Events-membership	
5 Cub scouts	
6 Boy scouts	
7 Girl scouts	
8 Little league	
9 Sport Interests	
10 Interests	
11 Favorite books	
12 Artwork	
13 Favorite teachers	
14 Memorable childhood events	
15 First job	
16 Marriage	
17 Business or life's work	
18 Hobbies/interests	
19 Proud accomplishments	

SUGGESTIONS	NOTES
20 Military service	
21 Inventions	
22 Education	
23 Favorite music	
24 Charities funded, volunteering	
25 Political or social values	
26 Unique personality traits	
27 Change of residence	
28 Birth of children	
29 Change of jobs	
30 Retirement	
31 Favorite quotes	
32 Later outlook on life	
33 Trips	
34 Loss of loved ones	
35 Remembering events	
36	
37	
38	
39	
40	
41	
42	
43	
44	
45	

Look for:

- *Pictures* of favorite vacations and events, such as marriage, graduation, or being with friends, can personalize and add value to the funeral or memorial services. Sometimes you can have pictures enlarged to poster size and displayed on an easel. These can be very useful in remembering your loved one during the best times of their life. Remembrance Films at 1-866-RNFILMS or www.RNFilms.com, can put together music and photos for a video.

- *Videos* or movies made of activities or interests to survivors. Short videos can be very touching and memorable. Most funeral homes and churches do not have video capabilities, but arrangements can be made for them.

- *Favorite Objects*, whether it is a book, baseball glove, music, trophy, or awards, these items can be put on display for either funeral or memorial services.

- *Places* for funerals and memorial should be considered based on the following criteria:

  > Ability to seat the number of people attending

  > Parking of vehicles

  > Handicap accessible

  > Music system/sound system/public address

  > A place to display pictures and memorabilia

  > A place to display flowers

  > Air conditioning where needed

- Alternate locations for funeral or memorial services:

  > Churches

  > Private residence

  > Knights of Columbus hall

  > University Music conservatory

  > Union hall

  > Township hall

  > Masonic lodge

  > Public park

Death Profiteering: The American Funeral Industry in Transition

Since prehistoric times, death has been followed by some sort of ritualized farewell. In more modern times, community members called morticians served to handle the physical needs of burial and to help support the emotional needs of their communities. However, large corporations have now frequently replaced the local mortician.

From its roots as a mom-and-pop trade, the American funeral industry has grown into a multi-billion dollar business. A handful of corporations own thousands of funeral homes and hundreds of the largest cemeteries.

Consumer behavior works against the establishment of new, independently owned funeral homes. Families return to funeral homes they previously used—whether or not the funeral home has been sold to a large conglomerate (consumers have no way of knowing) and without comparison-shopping for the best price and services. The fact that thirty-three percent of the time families choose a funeral home by location, without regard to price, is also a barrier to the new funeral home owner.

In many major metropolitan areas, corporations purchase well-established funeral homes that serve the same markets. Since the names of these funeral homes are rarely changed, the consumer has no clue that these businesses have been sold. Consumers who have made pre-arrangements with these firms are not told that the caskets and vaults previously selected may be substituted with "like" merchandise, since many of the corporations use different casket and vault suppliers. Quite often, the wholesale prices of merchandise and the quality of the product are not even close to what was originally selected and paid for.

Once a large corporation has acquired an established funeral home, the consumer is placed at a disadvantage. The locally owned firm, which was accountable to friends and neighbors in the community, has been replaced by a corporate owner more concerned with selling merchandise than serving the emotional needs of the bereaved. By heartlessly exploiting the emotions of the bereaved, which are under limited time constraints, the funeral industry has been very successful selling merchandise at higher profit margins than most other industries.

The American funeral industry is one whose consumers are naive, trusting people dealing with loss, sorrow, and sometimes guilt, who are not likely to comparison shop for funeral services. Seldom are prices or services compared and when they are, poorly informed consumers are at a great disadvantage for a number of reasons. With virtually no alternative sources for information other than funeral homes, most consumers are far less prepared to ask questions and inquire about alternative, less expensive merchandise or services.

To complicate price comparisons, identical caskets and vaults (which come from the same manufacturer) are given different names by competing funeral homes. When consumers do try to compare merchandise over the telephone, they cannot verify quality and usually must settle for vague descriptions of products. Another obstacle for the comparison shopper is the fact that the same corporation may own "competing" funeral homes, with different names. No wonder prices are similar!

Well-trained corporate sales tactics manipulate consumers towards the most expensive, profitable funerals. One of the best examples of corporate sales tactics involves "protective" caskets and vaults. "Protective from what?" you may ask while reading this book. But to someone suffering the sorrow of a recent loss of a loved one, a "protective casket and vault" can sound like a very good idea. These products do not stop the natural decomposition of human remains, yet the sales of both contribute a significant percentage to the industry's bottom line.

Another example of industry deceptiveness is the pre-paid or pre-need funeral contract. The funeral industry is aggressively selling pre-need funerals and memorials, using TV advertising, telephone solicitation, and direct mail. Corporations, privately owned funeral homes, cemeteries, casket manufacturers, and insurance companies all compete for sales of pre-need funeral services. Very few prepay contracts are written to the advantage of the consumer. Loopholes allow the seller to substitute merchandise and penalize the buyer for withdrawal or transfer to another funeral home. Few guarantee that your principal and interest will be refunded in full if you cancel. With high commissions paid to sellers of pre-need funerals, many promises of service and security of funds are made, but very few of these promises are in writing. Pre-need salespeople spend little time investigating a family's needs while pre-planning a funeral or memorial. They earn their commission by selling caskets, vaults, and "canned services," not by delivering personalized and meaningful memorials or funerals. With few exceptions, pre-selling is a scam that benefits the seller, not the buyer.

Let the buyer beware: The American Funeral Industry is failing in its pursuit to serve the emotional needs of the living, evident by the continued increase in demand for cremation without services. Few attempts are made to provide affordable, meaningful funerals or memorials that are assuring, uplifting, spiritual, and yes, even beautiful. There is a need for caskets, vaults, flowers, monuments, urns, and the funerals or memorials of which they are a part. Most of us need to express and share our loss and remember the one who has died. But the funeral has turned into a merchandising merry-go-round with corporate salespeople promising everything from "protection" to "perpetual care." Protecting for how long and from what? How long is perpetual? Who does this serve?

This guide is meant to be a straightforward source of information intended to give you, the consumer, the help you need when making funeral and memorial arrangements, comparing prices, and dealing with the slickest salespeople on earth. By showing you all of your options, without the influences of profit from caskets, vaults, funeral homes, cemeteries, or insurance sales, this guide will help you decide which services and merchandise to choose.

Thanks for the Memories . . .

Seldom are we able to express our feelings, expectations, philosophies, wishes, dreams and convictions to others before we die. Writing such a message may take more time and effort than what it takes to compare funeral and memorial service prices, but it will be worth it. For those who survive you, a few encouraging words, the thanks they may have never received, or simply "I love you". These words could be shared at the funeral or memorial service, or read privately if so desired. Such words can be treasures, passed on for generations to come, far more meaningful than letters etched on granite saying when you were born and died. A written note given to your children, grandchildren, special friends, significant others, will be cherished. Take the time and write what you want, seal the envelopes and set your mind at ease.

Glossary of Terms

*with consumer warnings

AIR TRAY

A container used to enclose a casket for airline shipping. Instead of purchasing a casket and air tray, you can buy a combination unit for use on all airlines. *

ALTERNATIVE CONTAINER

A cardboard or inexpensive wooden container used for cremation or immediate burial. All funeral homes have access to these. *

ARRANGEMENT CONFERENCE

A meeting between the funeral director and survivors, planning for burial, cremation, or body donation. During the arrangement conference, the funeral director should obtain information for: completing a death certificate; obituary (optional), explanation of service options, and selection of merchandise, if so desired, by the consumer. Before any information is taken or any services are planned, the General Price List, Casket Price List, and Vault Price List must be given to the family. *

ASHES

The end product of cremation, consisting of bone fragments reduced by extreme heat and pulverization. The purchase of an urn is not required by law; ashes are usually returned in a plastic bag which is placed inside a sturdy plastic box. If a funeral home or crematory insists on selling an urn, you can provide your own container for a fraction of the cost. *

AT-NEED ARRANGEMENTS

Arrangements made for burial, cremation, or body donation, after death has occurred, "at the time of need."

AUTOPSY

Medical procedure used to determine cause of death. An autopsy may be requested by a coroner, medical examiner, family physician, law enforcement official, or next of kin.

BASIC SERVICES OF FUNERAL DIRECTOR AND STAFF

Same meaning as the term "Professional Services of Funeral Director and Staff." Terms used to describe the services and minimum fees charged for: arrangement conference, completing and filing the death certificate, obtaining burial or cremation permits, completing veteran's and social security forms, writing an obituary (optional), and coordination of service options for burial, cremation, or body donation. This fee is usually not optional and is added to other fees that you may incur for the services you select. Prices vary considerably between funeral homes. Consumers should clearly understand what services are rendered and what they are paying for. You can expect these fees to be relatively high. *

CASKET PRICE LIST

Provided by funeral home, listing the caskets offered for sale or rent by their establishment. The price list should include a description of the casket and the retail price. Example: Pine casket with crepe interior $1500. If a casket has "protective" features, it should be listed as such. Make no assumptions about the quality of a casket or its ability to "protect" or delay decomposition, regardless of how much you pay. Many inexpensive, affordable caskets are readily available to funeral homes, but are not listed! When you compare prices, make sure you know the manufacturer and model numbers—funeral homes may change names to confuse shoppers. *

COLUMBARIUM

A structure or area in a mausoleum where ashes are placed. Individual units are called niches, capable of holding an urn.

COMBINATION SHIPPING CONTAINER
Used for airline shipping instead of purchasing a casket.

CREMAINS
See Ashes.

CREMATION
Process of burning the human body, reducing it to bone fragments and ash. Large bones that do not reduce by burning are pulverized into smaller fragments. Note: Law does not require the purchase of a casket and embalming and the purchase of an Urn is optional. * The ashes are returned to the family in a plastic bag, which is usually placed inside of a hard plastic box, adequate to hold the ashes until scattered or buried. If the funeral home insists that someone identify the deceased before cremation, the use of a gurney or embalming table would suffice.

CRYPT
An above ground unit or compartment in a mausoleum large enough to accommodate a casket, used in lieu of burial.

DEATH CERTIFICATE
A legal document that states where, when, and how a person died. It is the responsibility of the funeral home to gather this information and to have it signed by a doctor or medical examiner giving the cause of death. The completed certificate is filed with the county in which the person died. Certified legal copies are needed to collect insurance and transfer property, by probate court, banks, etc. Fees for certified legal copies vary between counties.

DIRECT BURIAL
No memorial or funeral services held prior to burial. Embalming and the purchase of a casket would be optional and not required by law in this case. An alternative container or rental casket could be used in lieu of purchasing a casket.

DIRECT CREMATION
No memorial or funeral services held. Embalming and purchase of a casket would be optional and not required by law in this case. An alternative container or rental casket could be used in lieu of purchas-

ing a casket. Note: Some funeral home require identification of the deceased before cremation and take that as an opportunity to sell cremation caskets or rental caskets. Viewing for identification can occur in an alternative container or cremation container, or on the dressing table of the funeral home.*

EMBALMING
The process of injecting preservative chemicals into the arterial system and draining the blood and fluids from the venous system. Instruments are used to pierce the internal organs and preservative chemicals are injected into the body's cavity to delay decomposition. Rarely is embalming done thoroughly enough to stop the natural process of decomposition, leaving many to question the importance of protective caskets or vaults.*

FUNERAL
A service, with the deceased present in a casket. Funerals are held for the benefit of the living, not the dead. With the use of music, religious messages, flowers, and the presence of friends and family showing concern, those grieving can begin the process of healing and acceptance, providing the closure needed by many.

FUNERAL HOME
A business selling merchandise and services related to the disposition of human remains through body donation, cremation, and burial. Services offered vary considerably. Many offer bereavement support groups and follow-up services such as: Assisting families with handling death certificates, transferring titles and property, bank accounts, and collecting insurance and pension benefits. Many funeral directors do offer creative services in planning and organizing memorials and funerals tailored to a family's needs, while others focus on sales and merchandising. Prices vary considerably and should be compared carefully.*

FUNERAL DIRECTOR
A businessperson who provides the services and merchandise necessary for body donation, cremation, and burial. Not to be confused with a psychologist when counseling is needed, or a lawyer when estate planning is required.

GENERAL PRICE LIST

Provided by funeral homes to any consumer requesting information on Pre-need or At-need Arrangements or services, without any obligation to buy. Required by law to be presented to consumers before any arrangements are discussed, and should include all charges for all services available. Some general price lists are intentionally made to be confusing, with complicated pricing structures, which make it difficult to compare to others. When needed, explain which services you desire, and have the funeral director give you a total for comparison. *

GRAVE LINER

Usually refers to the most basic, least expensive "vault or outer burial container" offered. It is what the casket is placed in at the cemetery. This is all that cemeteries usually require. Its primary function is to prevent the grave from collapsing, which creates additional maintenance for a cemetery. (See also Vaults).

IMMEDIATE BURIAL

See Direct Burial. No funeral or memorial services held.

IMMEDIATE CREMATION

See Direct Cremation. No funeral or memorial services held.

MAUSOLEUM

A building or structure for casketed human remains, used in lieu of burial. Some mausoleums have areas where services may be held, either committal rituals or simple funeral services. Individual spaces are called crypts. Usually very expensive and, once purchased, very difficult to resell at the price originally paid. *

MEMORIAL SERVICE

A service at which the deceased is not present in a casket. It can include the use of music, flowers, and religious message given by a member of the clergy. Memorial services can be held any time after death occurs, in a variety of places, with or without the use of a funeral director. Memorial services are often chosen over a funeral because they are less expensive. Since the timing of a memorial service offers more flexibility than a funeral, it is easier to plan.*

OBITUARY

A notice placed in a newspaper to notify the public that a death has occurred. It can include a picture of the deceased, accomplishments, memberships, life work, survivors' names (usually immediate family), the scheduled time for the funeral or memorial service, visitation, and a place where memorial contributions can be made.

"OTHER PREPARATION"

An expression used to describe the dressing, cosmetizing, and casketing of the deceased. There are usually two charges for preparation: embalming and "other preparation."

OUTER BURIAL CONTAINER

General description for any container in which a casket is placed for burial. No assumption should ever be made regarding quality, ability to protect, or delay human decomposition, regardless of what you pay. *

PRE-NEED ARRANGEMENTS

Process of planning prior to death for burial, cremation or body donation, with or without services being held. The benefits of pre-planning are: the ability to compare price, products, and services of funeral homes without time constraints or pressure, and the opportunity to closely examine the type of services and options available and to plan services accordingly. It does not have to include pre-payment. Funeral homes and cemeteries encourage pre-need payment because they are paid commissions for trusts and insurance sold.*

PRE-NEED INSURANCE

Similar to life insurance in that you can make one lump sum payment or spread payments over three, five, or ten years. During the payment period, you are covered for the services and merchandise selected. Penalties should be examined for cancellation or transfer to another funeral home or cemetery. When making payments, you will pay considerably more than the actual cost of services and merchandise. Remember, commissions are paid for the sales of merchandise and services, but not for planning without pre-payment.*

PRE-NEED TRUST ACCOUNTS

An interest-bearing account established with a financial institution to provide the money needed for funeral or memorial services at a later time. Trust accounts are established with one lump sum payment, at the current price of services and merchandise selected by the consumer. Interest and principal are used to offset any increases in prices and must not be withdrawn until death occurs. Fees can be charged for establishing a trust, canceling a trust, or transferring a trust to another funeral home. Some funeral directors will waive the fees considering that such goodwill will assure future business. Sales people are paid a commission on the amount of the trust established and will not usually waive these fees.*

"PROFESSIONAL SERVICES OF FUNERAL DIRECTOR"
See Basic Services of Funeral Director and Staff.

VAULT
A container in which the casket is placed for burial. No assumptions should be made regarding quality and ability to protect or delay human decomposition, regardless of what you pay. Vaults are primarily made of concrete with many optional features available. Some areas of the United States use steel, fiberglass, and plastic. Vaults can vary in quality, price, and ability to protect the casket. Prices should be carefully compared.

Body Donation Programs in the United States

ALABAMA

University of Alabama at Birmingham
School of Medicine, Department of Cell Biology
1530 3rd Avenue South, MCLM 690 0005
Birmingham, AL 34294-0005
205/934-0982

University of South Alabama
College of Medicine
Department of Cell Biology and Neuroscience
2042 Medical Sciences Building
Mobile, AL 36688
334/460-6490

ALASKA

Dr. Dennis Edwards, Academic Affairs
University of Alaska in Anchorage
3211 Providence Drive
Anchorage, AK 99508
907/786-1921

Human Gifts Registry
Wami Medical Education Program
University of Alaska
Fairbanks, AK 99701

ARIZONA

University of Arizona College of Medicine
Department of Cell Biology and Anatomy
Box 245044
1501 N. Campbell Avenue
Tucson, AZ 85724-5044
520/626-1801or 520/626-2097

Options for Arizona residents*
University of California at San Diego
Office of Learning Resources, M-011
School of Medicine
La Jolla, CA 92093
619/534-4536

*There is a transportation fee for all donors, even those who pass away within the State of Arizona.

Loma Linda University
Department of Anatomy
Loma Linda, CA 92354
714/824-4301

University of Nevada School of Medicine
Department of Anatomy
Manville Medical Sciences Building, Room 15
Reno, NV 89557-0046
702/784-6113

University of Utah College of Medicine
Department of Anatomy
401 Medical Education Building
50 North Medical Drive
Salt Lake City, UT 84132
801/581-6728

ARKANSAS

University of Arkansas for Medical Sciences
College of Medicine, Department of Anatomy
4301 West Markham Street #510
Little Rock, AR 72205-7199
501/686-5180

CALIFORNIA

University of California at San Diego
Office of Learning Resources, M-011
School of Medicine
La Jolla, CA 92093
619/534-4536

Loma Linda University
School of Medicine
24745 Stewart Street
Loma Linda, CA 92350
909/558-4301

UCLA School of Medicine
Department of Anatomy
UCLA Medical Center
10833 LE Conte Ave
Los Angeles, CA 90024-1763
310/825-9555

University of California, Davis
School of Medicine
Department of Cell Biology and Human
Anatomy
Davis, CA 95616
530/752-2100

University of California, San Francisco
School of Medicine, Department of Anatomy
513 Parnassus Avenue, Box 0452
San Francisco, CA 94143-0452
415/476-1861

CALIFORNIA continued

University of California, Irvine
Department of Anatomy
College of Medicine
Irvine, California 92697-1275
Phone: (714) 856-4548

Los Angeles College of Chiropractic Medicine
Department of Anatomy
6200 East Amber Valley Drive
Whittier, CA 90609-1166
231/947-8755 X252

University of Southern California
Keck School of Medicine
Department of Cell and Neurobiology
133 San Pablo Street, BMT 401
Los Angeles, CA 90089-9112
323/442-1881

Stanford University School of Medicine
1215 Welch Road, Modular #2
Stanford, CA 94305-5402
650/723-2404

Western University of Health Sciences
College of Osteopathic Medicine of the Pacific
Willed Body Program
Pomona, California 91766
Phone: (909) 469-5431

COLORADO

University of Colorado
School of Medicine
4200 East Ninth Avenue
Denver, CO 80262
303/315-7009

CONNECTICUT

University of Connecticut
School of Medicine, Department of Anatomy
263 Farmington Avenue
Farmington, CT 06030
203/679-2117

Yale University School of Medicine
333 Cedar Street
New Haven, CT 06510
203/784-2814

DELAWARE

NOTE: Delaware does not have any medical schools within the state. The two registry schools listed will retrieve within the state of Delaware.

Humanity Gifts Registry
Health Sciences Center
130 South 9th Street Suite 1455
Philadelphia, PA 19107
215/925-7469

Anatomy Board of Maryland
655 West Redwood Street
Room B-O26
Baltimore, MD 21201
303/547-1222

FLORIDA

Anatomical Board of the State of Florida
University of Florida
Health Science Center
P.O. Box 100235
Gainesville, FL 32610-0235
352/392-3588
1-800-628-2594 (Florida only)
Send E-Mail to the Anatomical Board

FLORIDA continued

University of Miami School of Medicine
Department of Anatomy
P.O. Box 016960
Miami, FL 33101
305/547-6691

GEORGIA

Emory University School of Medicine
Department of Cell Biology
1648 Pierce Drive
Atlanta, GA 30322
404/727-6230

Medical College of Georgia
1120 15 Street, Department of Anatomy
Augusta, GA 30912-2000
706/721-3731

Mercer University School of Medicine
1550 College Street
Macon GA 31207
912/752-4027

Morehouse School of Medicine
720 Westview Drive SW
Atlanta, Georgia 30310
404/752-1560

HAWAII

University of Hawaii at Manoa
John A. Burns School of Medicine
Department of Medicine
1960 East-West Road, Room T-311 Biomed
Building
Honolulu, HI 96822
808/956-7133

IDAHO

University of Idaho
Department of Anatomy
Student Health Building
Moscow, ID 83843
208/885-6696

Idaho State University
Anatomical Donations
Department of Biological Sciences
650 Memorial Drive
Pocatello, ID 83209-8007
208/282-4379
208/282-4150

ILLINOIS

Demonstrators Association
2240 West Fillmore Street
Chicago, IL 60612
312/733-5283

Southern Illinois University
School of Medicine
Carbondale, IL 62901
618/536-5511

INDIANA

Indiana State Anatomical Board
Indiana University School of Medicine
Department of Anatomy
Room 258, Medical Science Building
635 Barnhill Drive
Indianapolis, IN 46223
317/274-7450

IOWA

The University of Osteopathic Medicine
Health Science Anatomy Division
3200 Grand
Des Moines, IA 50312
515/271-1400

University of Iowa
College of Medicine
Department of Anatomy
1-470 Basic Science Building
Iowa City, IA 52242
319/353-5905

KANSAS

The University of Kansas
Department of Anatomy
College of Health Sciences and Hospital
39th at Rainbow Boulevard
Kansas City, KS 66013

KENTUCKY

The Body Bequeathal Program
University of Louisville School of Medicine
Department of Anatomical Sciences and
    Neurobiology
Health Science Center, Room A-916
Louisville, Kentucky 40292
TELEPHONE: 502/588-5165

University of Kentucky
Department of Anatomy
MN224 Chandler Medical Center
Lexington, KY 40536-0084
606/233-5276

KENTUCKY continued

Marshall University School of Medicine
(Eastern Kentucky and West Virginia)
Department of Anatomy
Huntington, WV 25701
304/696-3615

LOUISANA

Tulane University School of Medicine
Department of Anatomy
1430 Tulane Avenue
New Orleans, LA 70112
504/588-5255

Louisana State Anatomical Board
Louisana State University School of Medicine
Department of Anatomy
1901 Perdido
New Orleans, LA 70112
504/568-4012

LSU Medical School
Department of Anatomy
Box 33293
Shreveport, LA 70113
318/674-5314

MAINE

University of New England
College of Osteopathic Medicine
Department of Anatomy
11 Hills Beach
Biddeford, ME 04005
207/283-0171 x 335

MAINE continued

The University of Vermont
College of Medicine
Anatomy and Neurobiology
C427 Given Building
Burlington, VT 05405
802/656-2230

MARYLAND

Anatomy Board of Maryland
655 West Baltimore Street
Room B-026
Baltimore, MD 21201
410/547-1222

Uniformed Services
University of the Health Sciences
Multi-Discipline Laboratory
4301 Jones Bridge Road
Bethesda, MD 20014
202/295-3333

MASSACHUSETTS

Tufts University
School of Medicine
Department of Anatomy
136 Harrison Avenue
Boston, MA 02111
617/956-6686

Boston University School of Medicine
Department of Anatomy
80 East Concord Street
Boston, MA 02118
617/638-4245

MASSACHUSETTS continued

University of Massachusetts
Medical School
55 Lake Avenue North
Worchester, MA 01605
617/856-2460

Harvard Medical School
Department of Anatomy
25 Shattuck Street
Boston, MA 02115
617/732-1735

MICHIGAN

Wayne State University
School of Medicine
Department of Anatomy
540 East Canfield Avenue
Detroit, MI 48201
313/577-1188

University of Michigan Medical School
Department of Anatomy and Developmental
    Biology
3626 Medical Sciences, Building II
Ann Arbor, MI 48109-0016
734/764-4389
Web: http://www.med.umich.edu/anatomy

Michigan State University
Department of Anatomy
East Fee Hall, C-203
East Lansing, MI 48824
517/353-5398

MINNESOTA

Mayo Clinic
Section of Anatomy
Medical Science Building 3
200 First Street, S.W.
Rochester, MN 55905
507/284-2693

Department of Biomedical Anatomy
University of Minnesota at Duluth
School of Medicine
Duluth, Minnesota 55812

University of Minnesota
Bequest Program
321 Church Street, S.E.
Jackson Hall 4-135
Minneapolis, MN 55455
612/625-1111

(Seven County Area: includes Carver, Anoka, Dakota,
Hennepin, Ramsey, Scott, and Washington)
University of North Dakota
School of Medicine
Department of Anatomy
Grand Forks, ND 58202
701/777-2101
(N.W. Minnesota Only)

University of South Dakota
School of Medicine
Department of Anatomy
Vermillion, SD 57069
(S.W. Minnesota)

MISSISSIPPI

University of Mississippi
Department of Anatomy
Medical Center
2500 N. State Street
Jackson, MS 39216
601/984-1000

MISSOURI

The University of Health Science
College of Osteopathic Medicine
University Hospital
Department of Anatomy
2105 Independence Avenue
Kansas City, MO 64124
816/283-2000

University of Missouri School of Dentistry
& Kansas City School of Medicine
Department of Anatomy
2411 Holmes Street
Kansas City, MO 64108
816/231-0184

Washington University
School of Medicine
Department of Anatomy
660 South Euclid Avenue
St. Louis, MO 63110
314/454-5297

Department of Anatomy
St. Louis Inuversity
School of Medicine
1402 S. Grand Blvd.
St. Louis, Missouri 63104

MISSOURI continued

Kirksville College of Osteopathic Medicine
212 West Jefferson
Department of Anatomy
Kirksville, MO 63501
816/626-2468

Columbia School of Medicine
University of Missouri
Department of Anatomy M-304
Columbia, MO 65212
314/882-2288

MONTANA

Montana State University
Wami Medical Education Program
Bozeman, MT 59717
406/994-3230

University of North Dakota
School of Medicine
Department of Anatomy
Grand Forks, ND 58202
701/777-2101
(Eastern Montana)

NEBRASKA

State Anatomical Board
42nd & Dewey Avenue
Omaha, NE 68105
402/559-6249

University of South Dakota
School of Medicine
Department of Anatomy
Vermillion, SD 57069
605/677-5321
(N.E. Nebraska/along the border)

NEVADA

University of Nevada School of Medicine
Department of Anatomy
Manville Medical Sciences Bldg, Room 15
Reno, NV 89557
775/784-6908

University of California, San Diego
School of Medicine
Office of Learning Resources, M-011
La Jolla, CA 92093
619/452-4123

University of Utah College of Medicine
Medical Center
Salt Lake City, UT 84132
801/581-6728
(Eastern Nevada)

NEW HAMPSHIRE

Dartmouth Medical School
Department of Anatomy
Hanover, NH 03756
603/646-7636
WWW HomePage
E-Mail Response

NEW JERSEY

University of Medicine and Dentistry
of New Jersey
Department of Anatomy
185 South Orange Avenue
Newark, NJ 07103
201/456-4648

NEW JERSEY continued

UMDNJ-Robert Wood Johnson Medical School
Anatomical Association
675 Hoes Lane
Piscataway, New Jersey 08854-5635
800/GIFT-211 (800-443-8211)
www2.umdnj.edu/donorweb

NEW MEXICO

University of New Mexico —
    School of Medicine
Anatomical Donations Program
Department of Cell Biology and Physiology
Basic Medical Sciences Bldg. Room 159
Albuquerque, NM 87131-5218
505/272-5555
(Must be pre-registered)

NEW YORK

State University of New York
Upstate Medical Center
Department of Anatomy
766 Irving Avenue
Syracuse, NY 13210
315/464-5120
315/464-5047 (24 hr)

University of Rochester
School of Medicine
Department of Anatomy
Box 603
601 Elwood Avenue
Rochester, NY 14642
716/275-2592
716/275-2272 (24 Hr)

NEW YORK continued

State University of New York at Stony Brook
Department of Anatomical Sciences
Health Science Center
Stony Brook, NY 11794
516/444-3111 (24 Hr)

Columbia University College of
    Physicians & Surgeons
Department of Anatomy
630 West 168th Street
New York, NY 10032
212/305-3451 (24 Hr)

New York University College of Dentistry
Department of Anatomy
345 East 24th Street
New York, Ny 10010
212/481-5434
718/948-9269 (24 Hr)

State University of New York
Downstate Medical Center
Box 5, 450 Clarkson Avenue
Brooklyn, NY 100203
718/270-1014, 718/235-0505 or
718/277-7402 (24 Hr)

Cornell University Medical College
Department of Anatomy and Cell Biology
1300 York Avenue
New York, NY 10021
212/746-6140 (24 Hr)

NEW YORK continued

Mt. Sinai School of Medicine
Department of Medical Education
Annenberg Bldg, Room 1398
New York, NY 10029
212/241-7057 (24 Hr)

(Pre-registered only)
New York University School of Medicine
Department of Cell Biology
550 First Avenue
New York , NY 10016
212/263-5378

State University of New York at Buffalo
Health Science Center
Department of Anatomy 317 Farber Hall
Buffalo, NY 14214
716/831-2912
716/834-8128

New York Medical College
Basic Science Building
Valhalla, NY 10595
914/993-4025
914/735-4849 (24 Hr)

Albany Medical College
of Union University
47 New Scotland Avenue
Albany, NY 12208
518/445-5379
518/445-3125 (24 Hour)

NEW YORK continued

Albert Einstein College of Medicine*
Anatomical Donation Program
1300 Morris Park Avenue
Bronx, New York 10361
(718) 430-2847 (Monday–Friday)
(917) 556-2758 (Emergency)
*Transportation charge if more than 50 miles
from the college.

NORTH CAROLINA

Department of Anatomy
Bowman Gray School of Medicine
Winston-Salem, North Carolina 27103

Department of Anatomy
Duke University School of Medicine
Durham, North Carolina 27710

Department of Anatomy
School of Medicine
East Carolina University
Greenville, North Carolina 27834

Department of Anatomy
Medical Research Buidling
University of North Carolina at Chapel Hill
Chapel Hill, North Carolina 27514

NORTH DAKOTA

Department of Anatomy
Medical School
University of North Dakota
Grand Forks, North Dakota 58202

OHIO

Wright State University
School of Medicine
Department of Anatomy
Dayton, OH 45435
513/873-3067

Medical College of Ohio at Toledo
Department of Anatomy-C.S. 10008
P.O. Box 6190
Health Science Building
Toledo, OH 43699
419/381-4172

Ohio State University
College of Medicine
Anatomy Department
333 West 10th Avenue
Columbus, OH 43210
614/292-4831

Northeastern Ohio Universities
College of Medicine
Program of Human Anatomy
Rootstown, OH 44272
216/533-3476 x255

University of Cincinnati
College of Medicine
Department of Anatomy
231 Bethesda Avenue, M.L. 521
Cincinnati, OH 45267
513/558-5612

Ohio University
College of Osteopathic Medicine
Department of Anatomy
Athens, OH 45701
614/593-1800

OHIO continued

Case Western Reserve University
School of Medicine
Department of Anatomy
2119 Abington Road
Cleveland, OH 44106
216/368-3430

OKLAHOMA

Health Science Center
Anatomical Donation Program
University of Oklahoma
P.O. Box 26901
Oklahoma City, OK 73190
405/271-2424

Oklahoma College of Osteopathic Medicine
Department of Anatomy
1111 West 17th Street
Tulsa, OK 74107
918/582-1972 x346
918/496-9133

OREGON

University of Oregon
Health Sciences Center
Department of Anatomy
3181 SW Sam Jackson Park Road
Portland, OR 97201
503/225-7811
503/225-8311 (page)

PENNSYLVANIA

Humanity Gifts Registry
Health Sciences Center
130 South 9th Street, Suite 1550
Philadelphia, PA 19107
215/922-4440
Mailing address:
P.O. Box 835
Philadelphia, PA 19105-0835

Department of Anatomy
Hahnemann Medical College
230 N. Broad Street
Philadelphia, Pennsylvania 19102

Department of Anatomy
Milton S. Hershey Medical Center
Hershey, Pennsylvania 17033

Department of Anatomy
Jefferson Medical College
Thomas Jefferson University
1020 Locust Street
Philadelphia, Pennsylvania 19107

Medical College of Pennsylvania
3300 Henry Avenue
Philadelphia, Pennsylvania 19129

Department of Anatomy
Philadelphia College of Osteopathic Medicine
4150 City Line Avenue
Philadelphia, Pennsylvania 19131

PENNSYLVANIA continued

Department of Anatomy
School of Medicine
Temple University
3400 North Broad Street
Philadelphia, Pennsylvania 19140

Department of Anatomical Sciences
School of Dentistry
3223 North Broad Street
Philadelphia, Pennsylvania 19140

Department of Anatomy
School of Medicine
University of Pennsylvania
Philadelphia, Pennsylvania 19104

Department of Anatomy and Histology
School of Dental Medicine
University of Pittsburgh
Pittsburgh, Pennsylvania 15261

Department of Anatomy and Cell Biology
School of Medicine
3550 Terrace Street
Pittsburgh, Pennsylvania 15261

PUERTO RICO

Department of Anatomy
Ponce School of Medicine
G.P.O. Box 7004
Ponce, Puerto Rico 00731

Department of Anatomy
School of Medicine
University of Puerto Rico
G.P.O. Box 5067
San Juan, Puerto Rico 00936

RHODE ISLAND

Brown University
97 Waterman Street
Providence, RI 01912

SOUTH CAROLINA

Medical University of South Carolina
Department of Anatomy
171 Ashley Avenue
Charleston, SC 29425
803/792-3521

Gift Of Body Program
Dept. of Developmental Biology and Anatomy
School of Medicine
University of South Carolina
Columbia, SC 29208
Phone: 803/733-3369
803/777-7000—after hours and weekends only

SOUTH DAKOTA

University of South Dakota
School of Medicine
Department of Anatomy
Vermillion, SD 57069
605/977-5141
605/624-3932

TENNESSEE

University of Tennessee
Center for Health Sciences
Department of Anatomy
875 Monroe Avenue
Memphis, TN 38163
901/528-5965
901/529-5500

TENNESEE continued

Meharry Medical College
1005 8th Avenue North
Nashville, TN 37208
615/327-6308
615/244-0375

Vanderbilt University
School of Medicine
Department of Anatomy
21st Avenue South
Nashville, TN 37232
615/322-2134

Quillen-Dishner College of Medicine
Department of Anatomy and Cell Biology
Box 19960A
Johnson City, TN 37614-0002
423/439-4633
615/929-4480

TEXAS

Texas A & M University*
College of Medicine
Department of Anatomy
Medical Sciences Building
College Station, TX 77843
409/845-4913
409/822-1571
*Must live within 100 mile of College Station

University of Texas
Health Science Center
Department of Cell Biology
5323 Harry Hines Boulevard
Dallas, TX 75235
214/688-2221

TEXAS continued

Baylor College of Dentistry
Department of Anatomy
3302 Gaston
Dallas, TX 75246
214/828-8276

Texas College of Osteopathic Medicine
Department of Anatomy
Camp Bowie at Montgomery
Fort Worth, TX 76107-2690
817/735-2048
817/735-2210

University of Texas
Medical Branch at Galveston
Department of Anatomy
900 Strand Street
Galveston, TX 77550
409/761-1293
409/761-1101

Baylor College of Medicine
Department of Anatomy
1200 Morsund Avenue
Houston, TX 77030
713/798-4930

Department of Anatomy
Texas College Of Osteopathic Medicine
3516 Camp Bowie Blvd
Fort Worth, Texas 76107

University of Texas
Health Science Center
Department of Neurobiology and Anatomy
P.O. Box 20708
Houston, TX 77225
713/792-5703

TEXAS continued

Texas Tech University
School of Medicine
Department of Anatomy
Lubbock, TX 79430
806/743-2700
806/743-3111

University of Texas
Health Science Center
Department of Cellular and Structural Biology
7703 Floyd Curl Drive
San Antonio, TX 78284-7762

UTAH

University of Utah
College of Medicine
Department of Anatomy
401 Medical Education Building
50 North Medical Drive
Salt Lake City, UT 84132
801/581-6728
801/581-2121

VERMONT

University of Vermont
College of Medicine
Department of Anatomy and Neurobiology
Given Building, C-427
Burlington, VT 05405
802/656-2230
802/656-3473

Dartmouth Medical School
Department of Anatomy
Hanover, NH 03756
603/646-7640
603/646-5000

VIRGINIA

State Anatomical Progarm
9 North 14th Street
Richmond, VA 23219
804/786-2479

WASHINGTON

University of Washington
Department of Biological Structure
SM-20
Seattle, WA 98195
206/543-1860
206/328-3225

University of Washington
School of Medicine
Washington State University
WAMI University Site
Department of Anatomy
Pullman, WA 99164-3510
509/335-2602

WASHINGTON D.C.

Georgetown University Medical Center
School of Medicine
3900 Reservoir Road, NW
Washington, D.C 20007
202/687-1186

George Washington University
School of Medicine
Department of Anatomy
2300 I Street NW
Washington, D.C. 20037
202/994-3511

WASHINGTON D.C. continued

Howard University College of Medicine
Department of Anatomy
520 W Street, NW
Washington, D.C. 20059
202/636-6555

Uniformed Services
University of the Health Sciences
Multi-Discipline Lab
4301 Jones Bridge Road
Bethseda, MD 20014
202/295-3333

WEST VIRGINIA

Marshall University School of Medicine
Department of Anatomy
1542 Spring Valley Drive
Huntington, WV 25704
304/696-7382

West Virginia University Medical Center
Human Gifts Registry
Room 4052 Basic Science Wing
Morgantown, WV 26506
304/293-2212

Human Gifts Registry
West Virginia School of Osteopathic Medicine
400 Lee Street
Lewisburg, WV 24901
304/645-6270

WISCONSIN

University of Wisconsin
School of Medicine
Department of Anatomy
1300 University Avenue
Madison, WI 53706
608/262-2888
608/262-2800

The Medical College of Wisconsin
Department of Anatomy
8701 Watertown Plank Road
Milwaukee, WI 53226
414/257-8261

WYOMING*

University of Utah
College of Medicine
Department of Anatomy
2C 110 Medical Center
Salt Lake City, UT 84132
801/581-6728
801/581-2121
*Please note that Wyoming does not have a
medical school within the state.

About the Author

John M. Reigle earned a Bachelor of Independent Studies degree from the University of Michigan, Flint and a Mortuary Science degree from Wayne State University. He worked as a licensed funeral director and manager of the Colonial Chapel for Reigle Funeral Homes for 10 years. This was a business his grandparents, John J. and Wanda E. Reigle, started in Flint, Michigan in 1930. The family business, which had grown to include three funeral homes, a flower shop, and a limousine service, was sold in 1986 to Service Corporation International, the world's largest provider of funeral services. Reigle continued to work for SCI until 1993.

Since then he has been an advocate for consumer rights in the funeral industry. He believes the industry has failed professionally by not providing affordable, meaningful, valuable services to the living, and failed ethically, with several providers being cited for criminal and civil wrongdoing.

Reigle hopes that by writing *When Death Occurs: A Practical Consumer's Guide—Funerals, Memorials, Burial, Cremation, Body Donation* (© 2003) and giving educational seminars, he will encourage people to examine their options and plan services that are more meaningful to the living, with less emphasis on caskets, vaults, and urns. He removes the mystery from this secretive industry and gives the consumer the much-needed tools to help them comparison shop.

Reigle is currently working with Ron Choura of Michigan State University to build the Michigan State Experimental Telecommunications Site. It will provide broadband telecommunications service to eight counties in rural Northeastern Michigan and also provide service to areas that have never had phone service before.

Please contact me for information regarding
speaking, seminars, or consulting. 1-989-370-7116.

ORDER FORM
for
When Death Occurs:
A Practical Consumer's Guide

_____ book(s) at $19.95 each: _____

Sales Tax: _____
Please add 6% for products
shipped to Michigan

Shipping: _____
$4.00 for first book
$2.50 for each additional

TOTAL COST: _____

Telephone Orders: Call 1-989-370-7116

Email Orders: johnmyersreigle@usa.net

Postal Orders: Consumer Advocate Press, P.O. 64, Curran, MI 48728

Name _____

Address _____

City _____

State _____ Zip _____

Telephone _____

Email Address _____

Thank you for your order!